The Caribbean Irish

How the Slave Myth was Made

The Caribbean Irish

How the Slave Myth was Made

Miki Garcia

CHRONOS BOOKS

Winchester, UK
Washington, USA

JOHN HUNT PUBLISHING

First published by Chronos Books, 2019
Chronos Books is an imprint of John Hunt Publishing Ltd., No. 3 East St., Alresford,
Hampshire SO24 9EE, UK
office@jhpbooks.com
www.johnhuntpublishing.com
www.chronosbooks.com

For distributor details and how to order please visit the 'Ordering' section on our website.

ISBN: 978 1 78904 268 9
978 1 78904 269 6 (ebook)
Library of Congress Control Number: 2018958566

A CIP catalogue record for this book is available from the British Library.

Design: Stuart Davies

UK: Printed and bound by CPI Group (UK) Ltd, Croydon, CR0 4YY
US: Printed and bound by Thomson-Shore, 7300 West Joy Road, Dexter, MI 48130

Contents

'Do you know the Irish word for exile?'
'Please tell me,' she said.
'Deoraí.'
'How very interesting.'
'Maybe so, but do you know what it means?'
'No.'
'Deor means a tear and deoraí means one who has known tears.'
Colm Toibin, 'The South'

Doyle: 'Do you suppose a man need be a Celt to feel melancholy in Rosscullen? Why, man, Ireland was peopled just as England was; and its breed was crossed by just the same invaders.
Broadbent: 'True. All the capable people in Ireland are of English extraction.'
George Bernard Shaw, 'John Bull's Other Island'

'Being hanged in England is preferable to dying a natural death in Ireland.'
A quote by Frederick Douglass

Prologue

Every year, when St. Patrick's Day is getting closer, journalists across the globe start preparing feature articles about this world-famous patron saint of Ireland, a Roman boy from Wales who was supposedly snatched by Vikings in the late fourth century and brought to pagan Ireland as a slave (or arrived as a slave trader). Slavery had been around for centuries, long before England systematically had started the Atlantic slave trade. The fact that St. Patrick's Day has become the second most internationally-celebrated feast day after Christmas for all people regardless of backgrounds might be astonishing. The celebration of someone who became Irish through the extensive Irish diaspora is open to many interpretations. But this explains Ireland's intertwined history with Britain and certainly owes its success – politically and economically – to countless emigrants. Irish people had been visibly scattered all around the world but somewhat in disguise because they had always been part of the British Empire and some of them had even become British along the way.

The biggest St. Patrick's Day festival in the Caribbean is celebrated in Montserrat. Known as the Emerald Isle of the Caribbean, this tiny British Overseas Territory has a unique way of celebrating this day – a fusion of green and Caribbean Carnival. Outside Ireland, Montserrat and the Canadian province of Newfoundland and Labrador are the only two jurisdictions where St. Patrick's Day is a public holiday. But Montserrat is not the only Caribbean Island that celebrates this saint's day. So what is the Irish connection with the Caribbean? Why did the Irish end up there?

Because of the geographical proximity and historical connections, Irish history cannot be explained without the involvement of England. If you look at the map, Ireland's choices are limited by the Irish Sea as if it was a prisoner of geography.

The Anglo-Normans invaded Ireland in 1169 and England took control over Ireland in the 16th century. The 16th and 17th centuries were a conquest period and a catastrophic time for people in Ireland. As a consequence, a series of devastating events followed. The Tudor plantation of Ireland, and then Munster and Ulster plantations, Oliver Cromwell's nine-month sojourn, the 1641 Irish rebellion, the battle of the Boyne, amongst other ordeals. Demographic loss of local people and damage to infrastructure were enormous. What the English ultimately wanted was to turn Ireland into a Protestant nation. Anti-Catholic legislation had long existed in Ireland. Most notably, it was led by Henry VIII in the mid-16th century and Oliver Cromwell during the mid-17th century.

Because England ruled and colonised Ireland for such a long time, the process of turning the country English gradually and certainly seeped through the whole island. In fact, Ireland was (the North still is) the first colony of England, so it had been used for centuries as a ground for imperial experiments, such as rules, systems, norms, standards and the English language, not to mention how to handle rebellious people and what to do with them. These initiatives were initially tried out before being applied and confirmed on a global scale. The conquest of Ireland was the first step towards the English territorial expansion across the Atlantic and beyond.

Since occupying Ireland, Protestant English settlers had dispossessed the local Catholic people, depriving them of ownership or unfettered use of the land. By just being Catholics, they had no rights and were discriminated against, consequently leaving them in abject poverty. Local people resisted and the authorities constantly struggled to deal with them. The disastrous economic condition of Ireland during this period was caused by political events such as numerous battles and the unsettling political climate which produced a substantial number of so-called 'undesirable people'.

In the first decade of the 17th century, England started shipping labourers and settlers to develop their newly acquired colonies in mainland North America. With a little time lag, in the 1630s, indentured servants from the British Isles were transported to the British West Indies. This created a base for the subsequent indentured servant trade solidly enforced by Oliver Cromwell who changed the course of history. Because a substantial number of people went abroad from the British Isles, the 17th century has been coined as the period of English migration. England eventually used the newly obtained Caribbean colonies as dumping grounds for those rebellious people who didn't obey the authorities; prisoners of wars, criminals, landless 'proprietors', vagrants, widows, orphans and Catholic priests.

According to some estimates, as high as 70 percent of Irish people were indentured servants during this time. Indentured servants typically worked for a certain period of time and received land or sugar upon completion of their service. Although Irish people who were transported to the British West Indies were mostly indentured servants in scale and consequence, they were also planters, merchants and in-betweens. They were Catholic and Protestant people who left Ireland voluntarily, involuntarily or were forcefully transported. Between the mid-17th and the 18th centuries, the Irish were ubiquitous at every level of white society of the British West Indies. The words 'the Irish' cannot be generalised because they hailed from diverse social classes and occupational backgrounds. What's more, they didn't stay at the same level but moved up, and left and right. They were the most mobile and adaptable people as they changed sides, religions, status, names and allegiances depending on the way the wind was blowing. Just like with the politics of assimilation in Ireland, adaptability seemed to be ingrained in their culture as a survival mechanism within the British system. Irish people were colonised and colonisers both at home and abroad. As each other's closest neighbours, Ireland and Britain have a shared, long and complex history. Wherever the English went, the Irish were always with them. The Irish people were literally the backbone of the British colonies but at the same time, they tried to hinder the British Empire's colonial ambitions by aiding their enemies as soldiers of Spanish or/and French Forces or attacking British ships as pirates. For better or worse, Irish people have always acted as a catalyst on British politics.

Chapter 1

Before all that happened

Christianity arrived in Ireland in the early fifth century through the works of early missionaries. One of the most famous missionaries is Saint Patrick. In those days, Ireland was known as the centre of learning and literacy. Students from all across Europe came to the island to attend religious and medical schools, while Irish monks spread Christianity and literacy abroad. In post-Roman medieval Europe, slavery was not uncommon. In Anglo-Saxon England between the fifth and 11th centuries, slavery was linked with non-membership of the tribe. The Vikings raided the coasts of England, Wales and Scotland bordering the Irish Sea and slaves were moved across the sea from east to west. In 1169, the Anglo-Normans invaded Ireland and shortly conquered some parts of the country. A large number of people from England systematically arrived in Ireland. The Normans' attempt to establish feudalism was less successful than their conquest of England. Eventually, some Celtic rulers accepted King Henry II's over-lordship and the colonists steadily assimilated into the local inhabitants with Norman lords who became Celtic chieftains.

Four groups

By the 17th century, four major groups in Ireland had been identified: the native Irish who were descended from the pre-Norman inhabitants and were almost all Roman Catholic, the old English whose forebears had arrived during the Anglo-Norman invasion of Ireland in the 12th century who were mostly Catholic and royalist in politics, the new English who were Protestant settlers in Ireland from the 1580s onwards and the Scottish Presbyterians in Ulster.

The Pale

The Pale in the Dublin area where English kings had full control was created at the time of Henry II's expedition (1171-72). The term 'Pale' means boundary and 'beyond the Pale' implies 'uncivilised' or 'socially unacceptable'. The area of the Pale fluctuated in different time periods. The Normans controlled about three-quarters of Ireland by 1250. By the 14th century, Normans outside the Pale visibly integrated with local people in Ireland. This bothered the English and various laws were enacted. The Statutes of Kilkenny of 1366 forbade intermarriage between the Anglo-Normans and the Irish, banned religious bodies in English-controlled areas from accepting Irish people, banned the settlers from speaking Irish, and prohibited the adoption of Gaelic clothing and customs such as hurling.

English conquest

The first full conquest of Ireland by England between 1536 and 1691 officially established subordination of the country to Westminster. During the reign of Mary I in 1555, a large group of people from England were granted land in the new Queen's county, Laois. Sectarian animosity between Catholics and Protestants became extremely serious. Irish society had to be transformed from the clan-based Gaelic system to the state-governed and centralised English structure. During the English Reformation, the English, the Welsh and the Scottish accepted Protestantism, however, the Irish resisted and remained Catholic. The Tudor regime tried to incorporate Ireland into England along with Cornwall, Wales and Scotland. By 1641, the Plantation of Ulster had brought up to 80,000 English and Scottish settlers into the north of Ireland. Predominantly Presbyterian with a British and Protestant identity, the Ulster Scots were the foundation of the ruling class of prospective British administration in Ireland. The practice of Catholicism was banned and bounties were offered for the capture of Catholic priests.

Anti-Catholicism has a long and bloody history in Ireland. The roots of anti-Irish racism run deep. The English introduced a series of Penal Laws to disadvantage local Roman Catholic people. The religious schism stated that unless they converted to Protestantism, the native Irish and the Roman Catholic people were not able to hold power. Some of the reasons why the Protestant reformation didn't take hold amongst Irish people is that the government brutally exploited its resources and killed people, and used various inhumane methods to restrain the country. As a result, the Irish rebelled and resented the English and their rule. This English regime created a huge gap between the haves and have-nots, and as a result, ubiquitous Irish beggars.

Cromwell arrives

In 1641, an Irish Catholic rebellion broke in Ulster. Phelim O'Neill, Rory O'Moore, Lord Maguire and other leaders attacked and massacred a large number of Protestant settlers. The rebellion was soon joined by Irish Catholic lords and their followers and spread throughout Ireland except Dublin and Derry. The Irish rebels were initially successful and they were almost in charge of the whole country by 1642. But then, an English military officer Oliver Cromwell came to Ireland in 1649. Upon landing, Cromwell immediately took control over port cities on the east coast so that it was easier to facilitate the efficient landing of supplies and reinforcements from England. The first town to fall was Drogheda. Cromwell ordered that 'no quarter will be given'. The majority of the garrisons were destroyed, and tens of thousands of Catholic priests and civilians were killed.

According to *Oliver Cromwell's Letters and Speeches with Elucidations,* Cromwell wrote a letter after the killings of Drogheda in 1649:

> 'The next day, the other two Towers were summoned; in one of which was about six or seven score; but they refused to

> yield themselves: and we knowing that hunger must compel them, set only good guards to secure them from running away until their stomachs were come down. From one of the said Towers, notwithstanding their condition, they killed and wounded some of our men. When they submitted, their officers were knocked on the head; and every tenth man of the soldiers killed; and the rest shipped for the Barbados. The soldiers in the other Tower were all spared, as to their lives only; and shipped likewise for the Barbados...I am persuaded that this is a righteous judgement of God upon those barbarous wretches who have imbrued their hands in so much innocent blood; and that it will tend to prevent the effusion of blood for the future – which are the satisfactory grounds to such actions, which otherwise cannot work but remorse and regret...It hath pleased God to bless our endeavours at Drogheda...The enemy were about 3,000 strong in the town...I do not think 30 of the whole number escaped with their lives. Those that did are in safe custody for the Barbados...I wish that all honest hearts may give the glory of this to God alone, to whom indeed the praise of this mercy belongs.'

Cromwell himself estimated that approximately 2,100 were killed but some historians believe that the number could be up to 3,600. Cromwell's New Model Army took Trim, Dundalk, Carlingford, Newry and several other towns in the North. Then, Cromwell's troops progressed to the south and secured more ports. His next target was Duncannon in Wexford. Then, they moved on to Waterford, Tipperary, Limerick and Galway. Local people fought bloody battles and resisted but eventually surrendered.

Tories

The local landlords whose properties had been seized and

refused to transplant were known as the Tories. The English government adopted stringent methods to hunt them down. The Cromwellians distinguished in their rewards for information or capture of outlaws between private and public Tories. Irish people themselves were recruited to track down and kill or capture the Tories and bounties were offered to those who became collaborators. Parliamentary commanders were ordered to capture Tories and execute them along with those civilians who assisted them. Major Morgan, MP for Wicklow, described on 10 June 1657 how the Irish were treated: 'We have three beasts to destroy...that lay burdens upon us. The first is the wolf on whom we lay five pounds a head if a dog, and ten pounds if a bitch; the second beast is a priest, on whose head we lay ten pounds, and if he is eminent more. The third beast is the Tory, and on his head, if he be a public Tory, we lay ten pounds, and if he is a private Tory, we pay 40 shillings.'[1]

Colonel Lawrence, the chief commissioner in Loughrea wrote on the atrocious situation of the Tories: 'The Irish had been driven from garrisons, castles, and places of strength to bogs and woods. There they lurked, watching for opportunities to commit murders and outrages...Sundry persons were daily taken out of their houses in the night time and sometimes set upon as they travel upon the highway, or are surprised by these desperate persons, and carried into woods and bogs, and there murdered or kept in a miserable manner, in cold, nakedness, and hunger, and their houses burned, and their goods carried away until they pay a ransom.'[2]

Transportation of the unwanted

After the storming of Drogheda and other towns, the suppression of large-scale opposition in Ireland by the English army under Cromwell led to the dispatch of prisoners and ordinary people and the policy of transportation became a common method to handle rebel soldiers and prisoners. Cromwell had two objectives. To place Ireland under English control and to confiscate the land. In order to achieve these, he imposed an extremely harsh settlement on the Irish. Those who participated in the rebellion of 1641 were executed, captured ones were transplanted in Connaught and Clare, or transported to the Caribbean. Cromwell also ordered the surviving members of the garrison to be shipped to Barbados. Over the coming years, thousands of military prisoners were removed.

In 1652 and 1653, the English parliament passed the policy known as 'To Hell or Connaught'. The English parliament planned to seize three-quarters of Ireland. They drove the populations of Ulster, Munster and Leinster into an area west of the River Shannon. The offence could be simply 'being there'. The way it worked was that if the Irish were found east of the Shannon, they would be killed as a penalty, or tried and convicted of 'being at large and sentenced to perpetual banishment, and be sent into America or some other parts beyond the seas', then typically pardoned for the British West Indies. The authorities in Dublin welcomed this move because they were concerned by the 'great multitudes of poor swarming in all parts of this nation'. England also periodically emptied the jails throughout Ireland by sending them across the Atlantic.

Along with political prisoners, the English authority openly admitted that men-catchers were hired to delude destitute and wandering people with force or false promises to put them on board their ships. So-called 'unwanted' children and grown-ups were kidnapped by press-gangs while asleep or off the street. For instance, in 1654, the Governors of Carlow, Kilkenny, Clonmel, Wexford, Ross and Waterford had orders to arrest and deliver to Captain Thomas Morgan, Dudley North and John Johnson, English merchants, 'all wanderers, men and women and such other Irish within their precincts as should not prove they had such a settled course of industry as yielded them a means of their own to maintain them, all such children as were in hospitals or workhouses, all prisoners, men and women, to be transported to the West Indies'. They were guarded by the governors and taken to the ports for shipping. But all detainees were provided for and maintained by contractors or agents. None of them were discharged without the governor's permission.

Displacement

After the Cromwellian conquest of Ireland, his policy of the displacement of the Irish population became a common practice. In 1652, the Act for the Settlement of Ireland was issued which imposed penalties including death and land confiscation against participants and bystanders of the Irish Rebellion of 1641 and subsequent unrest. It detailed the fate of Ireland and its people: 'that it is not the intention of the Parliament to extirpate that whole nation, but that mercy and pardon, both as to life and estate, may be extended to all husbandmen, ploughmen, labourers, artificers, and others of the inferior sort, in manner as is hereafter declared; they submitting themselves to the Parliament of the Commonwealth of England, and living peaceably and obediently under their government...' The second clause excluded all Catholic clergy from pardon. As a result, hundreds were killed or banished overseas: 'That all and every Jesuit, priest, and other person or persons who have received orders from the Pope or See of Rome, or any authority derived from the same, that have any ways contrived, advised, counselled, promoted, continued, countenanced, aided, assisted, or abetted; or at any time hereafter shall any ways contrive, advise, counsel, promote, continue, countenance, aid, assist, or abet the rebellion or war in Ireland, or any the murders or massacres, robberies, or violence committed against the Protestants, English, or others there, be excepted from pardon for life and estate'. And the next clause listed hundreds of people who were killed or banished overseas namely James Butler, Earl of Ormond, James Touchet, Earl of Castlehaven, Ulick Bourke, Earl of Clanricarde, Christopher

Plunket, Earl of Fingal, James Dillon, Earl of Roscommon, Richard Nugent, Earl of Westmeath, Morrogh O'Brien, Baron of Inchiquin, Donogh MacCarthy, Viscount Muskerry, Theobald Taaffe, Viscount Taaffe of Corren and Richard Butler, Viscount Mountgarret.

Although the Cromwellian conquest of Ireland ended in 1653, a score of rebels could be still found all across Ireland. By the time an Act for the Attainder of the Rebels in Ireland was issued in 1657, hundreds of thousands of people had already been transported to the Caribbean or been sent to join foreign armed forces services.

The clearing of whole populations, or the ethnic cleansing of an entire people, was not common in early modern Europe. The Lords of the Council ordered Lord Ormonde, lieutenant general of the army in Ireland, 'to burn, spoil, waste, consume, destroy and demolish all the places, towns and houses where the said rebels are...and to kill and destroy all the men there inhabiting able to bear arms'.[4] Sir Bulstrode Whitelocke, an English lawyer and a member of the House, believed that the Irish would be rooted out by a new and overwhelming plantation of England and that another England would be speedily found in Ireland.

Banishment legislation had existed long before Cromwell conquered Ireland and it was largely aimed at the Irish. It was not only in Ireland but in England, too. For instance, in 1594, all Irish people who looked more like refugees were ordered to leave England. A large number of Irish vagrants and other victims of kidnapping and deception visibly existed throughout England. During this period vagrancy laws that existed legitimately allowed for a large number of destitute people to be transported. The fact that hundreds of thousands of Irish men serving as soldiers at home and abroad meant that vulnerable groups namely widows and children were left behind. As a 'means of clearing the country of vagrants', they were all removed and shipped to the British colonies.

Although there were laws against vagabondage since the 14th century, they were rather too vague in terms of logistics. That's why the Irish were transported by agents and merchants and no complete official records exist although there are some random entries in the state papers as the Council issued orders to 'transport the Irish' throughout the 17th century. It is impossible to tell who were forced, voluntary migrants, or to define vagabonds, criminals and the judicial processes.

Wandering Irish

From the late Tudor period, poor Irish people had been regularly removed. In the early 17th century, there were four groups that could be identified as rogues in England: the professional rogues; wandering pedlars; runaway apprentices/servants; and the Irish. An observer noted about the Irish: 'Nineteen of them were punished as vagrants in Salisbury between 1629 and 1633 when Irish famine pushed hundreds of emigrants into the western counties. They were more conspicuous than their numbers suggest, since they often moved in bands of dozen or more'.[5]

Ever since England took over Ireland and their sufferings started, Irish people went through numerous famines and wars. Because the famine in 1633 created a score of people leaving Ireland, Charles I issued a proclamation in 1633 for 'the speedy sending away of the Irish Beggars out of this Kingdom into their own country and for the Suppressing of English rogues and vagabonds according to our laws'. This gave Irish beggars 40 days to leave England or they would be punished as rogues and vagabonds, and then sent back to Ireland.

When fighting started against the English administration in Ireland in 1640 and with the Irish rebellion in 1641, then the civil wars, wandering Irish refugees in England became a common sight. In particular, parishes in Gateshead, North-East England, recorded that they took many families during this period. The thirteen years' war, from 1641 to 1654, followed by the departure of 40,000 Irish soldiers with the chief nobility and gentry to Spain, had left behind a large number of widows and deserted wives with destitute families, and the others with no visible means of livelihood. In 1690, the defeat of the pro-Roman Catholic Stuart King James II produced more wandering Irish people and pushed them out of the country.

Demographic disaster

Cromwell is responsible for a demographic disaster in the mid-1600s in Ireland as he caused massive casualties and deportations amongst the local population. His conquest of Ireland was defined by its cruelties and characterised as ethnic and religious cleansing as it sought to wipe out all Irish Catholics. Some historians called it a genocide. The Cromwellian conquest was a turning point in Irish history as it destroyed the native Irish Catholic landowning classes and completed the British colonisation of Ireland. Ireland was forcefully merged into the Commonwealth of England and Scotland.

By 1650, Ireland had been completely destroyed as Cromwell's soldiers suppressed most of the areas. Estimates vary depending on historians. For instance, an English economist William Petty estimated that the death toll of the wars in Ireland since 1641 was more than 618,000 people, or about 40% of the country's pre-war population. Of these more than 400,000 were Catholics, 167,000 killed directly by wars or famines and the rest by war-related diseases such as plague. Ireland's population was about 1,500,000 in 1641 and it was halved in 1651. On top of these casualties, about 54,000 Irish soldiers who fought in the Confederate and Royalist armies left the country to find service in the armies of France or Spain, according to the estimate by William Petty. Many clergymen also fled to continental European countries. Additionally, up to 100,000 people, the majority of them destitute and beggars were transported to English colonies in the Caribbean and mainland America.

Following the victory of his New Model Army, Cromwell described Ireland as a 'clean paper'. Within four years, Ireland was completely transformed. Because the deportation of the most population from Ireland to the Caribbean was quite substantial, it is called 'the Green Atlantic' and Irish republican and socialist leader James Connolly described it 'the Via Dolorosa of the Irish'.[3] The financial losses of the war in Ireland during this period were massive. It was estimated to be around 10,355,000 pounds.

Landlord system

In order to clear the whole population of Ireland, the Army Council debated whether to 'eradicate the natives' or merely 'to divest them of their estates'.[6] In the end, they undertook both and achieved their goals for the most part. Because the surviving Irish were forcibly removed, the most land became available for mass settlement for Cromwellian officers, soldiers from England and general English and Scottish settlers.

During this period, almost 40 percent of the land was taken from local Catholics and given to parliamentarian soldiers who served in Ireland. They received an allotment of confiscated land as wages. As a result, hundreds of thousands of New Model Army veterans settled in Ireland. Those surviving Catholics who were not sent westward lost everything and had to work for the new landowners. Under the Adventurers Act which was passed in 1640, those who lent money to Parliament for the subjugation of Ireland would also be paid in confiscated land in Ireland.

Although they were allocated land in Ireland, some soldiers didn't actually stay because they simply didn't want to remain in Ireland, didn't want to be farmers or both. In some cases, the land was not suitable for cultivation and many of them eventually sold their allotments to make money or/and rented. The landlord system had begun.

Travellers

Their true origins were not exactly known, although their own language Shelta is believed to have existed as far back as the 13th century. Historians and scholars suggested various theories that Irish Travellers might be: descended from a race of pre-Celtic minstrels; a nomadic population of refugees from when the Plantation of Ulster began in the late 1500s; descended from those Irish who were displaced during Oliver Cromwell's campaigns; a nomadic population of refugees during the great hunger of the potato famine of the 1840s. However, the latest study by the Royal College of Surgeons in Ireland, University College Dublin and the University of Edinburgh that came out on 10 February 2017 reveals that it has confirmed that Irish Travellers were separated from the main settled population in Ireland approximately 360 years ago, during the mid-1600s. According to DNA analysis, researchers tracked the Traveller community to between eight and 14 generations ago, to roughly the period when Cromwell came to Ireland. He thought the most barren land to farm in Ireland was in the west, Connaught. Anyone who refused to give up their land to English soldiers would get killed or sent to the west of Ireland, hence, his own quote 'To Hell or Connaught'. Irish travellers are the descendants of those people who were pushed away to the west and escaped the ordeal, and were forced to be nomadic in their own land.

For the last time

In 1690, the Battle of the Boyne was fought which was the last time two crowned kings of England, Scotland and Ireland faced each other. The battle between William of Orange, a Dutch protestant who had recently been jointly crowned monarch of England, Scotland and Ireland and Catholic James II took place across the River Boyne near Drogheda. William of Orange won the battle which secured the Protestant ascendancy in Ireland. Between the mid-16th and the early 17th century, plantations were systematically implemented. Scottish and English Protestants settled as colonists in Ireland, mainly in the provinces of Munster, Ulster and the counties of Laois and Offaly.

Timeline

The history of Ireland is often defined by internal migration and emigration. And the root cause of the diaspora has been always English rule in Ireland. The Irish Diaspora in the Caribbean stretched through different time frames, different geographical locations and different group of individuals. Royalist conspirators, prisoners and other criminals were also sent from across the British Isles but the large majority of them were transported from Ireland.

Before the systematic Atlantic slave trade from an African continent began, England transported a large group of people from Ireland. England learned how to transport convicts and the so-called 'unwanted' during this period. By 1700, the indentured servant trade to the British West Indies had dwindled, but Britain started applying what it had learned in Australia, the official penal colony as it was made the principal destination for convicts, vagrants and orphans from Ireland. Even after the British slave trade officially ended, Britain was still transporting Irish people from Ireland and other regions to Australia until 1868 in the name of establishing a new colony, as well as to South Africa, albeit in a more efficient and improved way.

1623 St Christopher becomes the first English colony in the Caribbean

1627 Barbados becomes an English colony

1632 Montserrat and Antigua become English colonies

1641 Outbreak of the Irish Rebellion

1649 Cromwell's invasion of Ireland and transportations begin after the storming of Drogheda. Transplantation to Connacht begins

1650-54 Catholic troops exiled to the Continent
1655 Jamaica becomes an English colony
1658 Death of Cromwell brings an end to mass transportations
1660 Restoration of Charles II
1662 Act of Settlement
1680 Last of indentured servants on Barbados freed
1690 The Battle of the Boyne

Chapter 2

Life in the Tropics

Ireland might not have produced internationally well-known explorers but being an island, they know the ocean very well as they have been sailing far and wide. Legend has it that when Christopher Columbus stopped in Galway on the way to America in 1490, he picked up some Irish sailors who accompanied him to the Caribbean.

Independent Irish colonists, migrants and adventurers had been living in various islands in the New World who had been hunting livestock and growing tobacco before the English started colonising the region. Small-scale independent Irish settlers were making a living throughout the Caribbean. For example, there were some Irish pioneers living in St. Lucia by 1605 and Grenada in 1609. 'A noble gentleman of the house of the Earl of Thomond', Bernard O'Brien was the one of the first Irish slave owners in the New World.[7] In 1612, at least 14 Irishmen were present in a stockade trading post on the Tauregue River and a group of Irish settlers were living in the Guiana (Amazon). Born in 1603, the native Gaelic speaker O'Brien crossed the Atlantic at 17-year-old to become a planter in the Amazonian tobacco colony. Irish planters Philip and James Purcell also founded a tobacco colony on the Amazon.

In the Caribbean, the English were not the first comers from Europe. They initially started establishing their own settlements where the Spanish had not colonised. St Christopher (St. Kitts) became the first English colony in 1623, then Barbados in 1627, Nevis in 1628, Montserrat and Antigua in 1632, Jamaica in 1655, amongst other islands. These colonies in the Caribbean became the British West Indies. Britain, at this stage England, was constantly fighting against other European powers and struggling to obtain more territories. So they decided to focus on St Christopher, Barbados, Nevis, Antigua, Montserrat and Jamaica.

Between 1641 and 1652, it is estimated that up to 504,000 people were disappeared from Ireland by wars, plague, famines, poverty and banishment. As is customary, the Irish travelled around the world and settled with the British. By the mid-17th century, the Irish were ubiquitously seen throughout the British West Indies. The majority of the Irish in the Caribbean were Catholic people from southern Ireland. Most of them were indentured servants, craftsmen and a small affluent minority people who paid their own passages and arrived to make a living or fortune. Some of them were auctioned by planters and administrators upon arriving, while the others arrived with contacts in advance. After Cromwell's unprecedented scale and speed of transporting, however, the treatment indentured servants received started becoming inhumane.

As the people had to go through constant wars, conflicts and poverty in Ireland, the English authorities and wealthy people justified themselves by saying that transporting them out of Ireland was in their interest. Joseph Williams, the author of *Whence the Black Irish of Jamaica*, wrote that transportation of Irish people to the British West Indies was 'a measure beneficial to Ireland, which was thus relieved of a population that might trouble the planters; it was a benefit to the people removed, who might thus be made English and Christians; and a great benefit to the West Indian sugar planters, who desired the men and boys for their bondmen, and the women and Irish girls in a country where they had only Maroon women and Negresses to solace them'.

At one point, Irish people consisted of the majority within the British West Indies, but the population started decreasing along with the increasing number of slaves from Africa. In many ways, the influx of African people drew a visible line between slaves and indentured servants. As the slave population started taking over Irish servants' work, Irish people climbed up the social ladder by acquiring land, their own slaves and status and by being elected and appointed to the Council or Assembly.

Push factors

People left Ireland and migrated for a number of reasons. Push factors are those which force a person to leave, while pull factors are those which encourage a person to migrate.

Cromwell

Following the 1641 rebellion and the rise of Oliver Cromwell and during and after the English Civil War (1642-1651) which stemmed from conflict between Charles I and Parliament over an Irish insurrection, several thousand rebels, royalist supporters and ordinary people were transported across the Atlantic. Although England had been sending indentured servants to mainland American colonies and the Caribbean before Cromwell's conquest of Ireland, he set a new standard of the way to handle 'undesirable people'.

Lawful transportation

New regulations in the early 1650s in Ireland further pushed people to leave Ireland as the English started forced transportation en masse. A proclamation stating that all laws in force in England for the punishment of rogues and idle people was enforced in Ireland. As various warrants were granted during this period, governors, soldiers and merchants were in charge of this procedure. According to a letter from the English authority, the governor of Waterford was to transport local prisoners to the Caribbean in 1652; Bristol merchants transported 400 Irish Tories from any ports in Ireland to the Caribbean islands in January 1654; Sir John Clotworthy transported 500 'natural Irishmen' to America in April 1653; on September 24, 1653, a State Paper noted a licence was issued to Richard Netherway of Bristol to transport 100 Irish Tories from Ireland to Virginia; London merchants also took 300 Irishmen; the English authority further ordered governors of Carlow, Kilkenny, Clonmel, Wexford, Ross and Waterford to deliver all local vagrants to Captain Thomas Morgan, Dudley North, and John Johnson for transportation; all vagrants in Limerick and Cork were handed over to Captain John Norris in April 1654; sixty women from Connaught were handed over to Colonel Stubbers in June 1654; John Mylam, merchants was in charge of all prisoners in Clonmel, Waterford, Wexford, Kilkenny and Carlow.[8]

In November 1653, the Commissioners of Parliament for the Affairs of Ireland ordered Colonel Edmund O'Dwyer to transport priests, Jesuits and other persons in Popish orders who were still in Ireland. Oliver Cromwell wrote to Charles Fleetwood, Lord Deputy of Ireland: 'Some merchants of the city of Bristol having petitioned to me for licence to transport 400 of the Irish Tories, and such other idle and vagrant persons as may be thought fittest to be spared out of Ireland, for planting of the Caribbee Islands, which address of theirs I do recommend to your consideration that their desire therein may be granted in such a way as to you shall seem fit and expedient'.[9] Wars and political instability produced a high number of vagabonds. In April 1654, all vagabonds in Cork and Limerick were sent to Captain John Norris and his agents for transportation. In June 1654, Col. Stubbers was ordered to transport Irish women who were vagrants, idlers and wanderers in Connaught and then in January 1655, Catholic priests in custody in Dublin who were not found guilty of murder were transported to Barbados.

Penal laws

The political climate was one of the factors that pushed the people out of Ireland. The accession of William III in 1689 enacted several versions of the penal laws. This meant that for Catholics to hold public office, other official positions and certain professions became almost impossible and all kinds of opportunities were limited for them as long as they were in Ireland.

Unemployment

The whole system in Ireland was designed to make Catholic people underprivileged. The Navigation Act of 1663 made the Irish officially forbidden to share in the victualling of ships engaged in the plantation trade. Beef exportation to England was also banned. The woollen trade started to look promising to compete with the English market but a series of acts that were created after 1698 made it impossible. Irish artisans couldn't find enough jobs in the linen industry either. Farmers couldn't get away from rack-renting absentee landlords. It was a vicious cycle.

Famines

Various famines, the most serious ones in 1670, 1725, 1726 and 1727, hit the already impoverished people hard. For instance, during the early 1670s, livestock diseases and poor harvests constantly occurred in Munster. The Quaker missionary William Edmundson in Ireland witnessed and wrote: 'several families that had lived plentifully...their corn being spent and cattle dead...shipped themselves for servants to the West Indies to get food'.

Pull factors

Irish Governors

Quite a few Irish people assumed the positon of local officers and governors and they often encouraged their country people to settle in the British West Indies. The most prominent Irish governor was Tipperary man William Stapleton who brought settlers from Ireland and encouraged them to obtain certain professions and land. He first arrived in Barbados with Tobias Bridge and his regiment in 1667. At the time, the governor of Barbados was Lord Willoughby and Stapleton was given the rank of lieutenant colonel. Shortly Stapleton was promoted to become deputy Governor of Montserrat (1668-1671) as a member of the first Leeward Island federation and then Governor of the Leeward Islands (1672-1685) who managed St Christopher, Nevis, Montserrat and Antigua. He urged capable Irish people to purchase abandoned plantations. Moreover, Stapleton built two parish churches and obtained Montserrat's first resident Anglican clergyman. He married Anne Russell, the daughter of Colonel Randolph Russell, a Protestant heiress from the ruling English elite on Nevis. This enabled him to establish good contacts with wealthy planters across the Leeward Islands. He acquired a plantation on Montserrat and a property on St Christopher for himself. By using his power, he also granted plantations on Nevis and Antigua to his family members and friends. His two sons also obtained properties in Montserrat and Antigua, while his two daughters were married to prominent Irish men in the Caribbean. His brothers Redmond and John were also appointed deputy governors of Montserrat. When Stapleton took over as governor of Montserrat, the Lords of Council described him as: 'a gentleman of known valour and integrity and born in Ireland and therefore understands the better to govern his countryman'.

Work and land

By working as indentured servants, they hoped to make a living and obtain land at the end of the contract. There were plenty of work opportunities because newly acquired British West Indian islands needed to be developed. Ships were readily available as they were crossing the Atlantic on a regular basis in order to conduct the triangular trade. Sometimes, planters and colonists were individually ordered to bring more labourers.

Indentured labourers were always necessary in English colonies. Quite a few Irish people worked both on the North American mainland and in the Caribbean. For example, the Lord Proprietor of Carolina wanted to obtain some servants and asked a servant trader in 1669 to 'sail with all possible speed' for Kinsale in Ireland. He instructed the trader to obtain a cargo of servants and to fill the ship with Irish provisions and set sail for Barbados, where all the provisions were sold. Sugar was purchased there and upon arriving in Carolina, the servants and sugar were dropped off. In the 1660s, colonists in Carolina paid higher prices for servants than those in Barbados therefore merchants often by-passed the West Indian market. As captains had to fill the ship, sometimes the vessels had to change direction either to mainland American colonies or the Caribbean. Although depending on the year, the Caribbean was generally more popular and early passengers often demanded that the captain take them where they wanted to travel.

Chain migration

Some migrants arrived with capital and skills – namely the sons of the Galway tribes, old English gentry and merchant families. In the majority of cases, wealthier people arrived to conduct more profitable trading business through kinship networks. Irish migrants were scattered all across the Caribbean and North American colonies.

How many were there?

Although the British West Indies received a large influx of Irish settlers, no one knows exactly how many Irish people were transported. There are no official written records on exact numbers even though state papers continuously issued orders of transportation. Statistics and estimates vary as some of them include mainland American colonies or other people from the British Isles such as Scottish and English people. As is always the case, Irish people are not homogenous. They were Catholics (native Irish and old English) and Protestants (new English and Ulster-Scots), general indentured servants, convicts, as well as planters, colonial administrators and merchants.

An English economist William Petty estimates that one sixth of the adult males, some 34,000 men were transported out of Ireland and sold abroad in the aftermath of the 1649 conquest. Some historians suggest up to 60,000 Irish people were sent to the British West Indies by Cromwell around the 1650s. Between 1651 and 1660, it is estimated that up to 130,000 Irish people were transported to mainland America and the British West Indies. Another estimate suggests that there were around 190,000 white migrants before 1660 in the British West Indies and the mainland colonies while another report indicates between 4,000 and 12,000 were Irish people around this period.

According to another calculation, up to 12,000 Irish people had been present in the British West Indies by 1660 when there were about 50,000 African slaves. Moreover, a mobile population namely Irish soldiers and sailors also arrived in the Caribbean directly and indirectly from Ireland who were thought to have numbered up to 50,000. Various estimates suggest, those who were sent to the Caribbean and mainland American colonies were ranged between 50,000 and 100,000 from the Transportation Act in 1718 to the outbreak of the American Revolution in 1765.

Although there were indentured servants from Scotland and England, the Irish made up the largest part of this group. A report by Carl and Roberta Bridenbaugh wrote: 'despite meager evidence it is difficult not to conclude that in the English West Indies in 1650, the Irish settlers constituted more than half of the entire population'.

Because the disposal of vagrants and criminals by transportation became an English custom, Irish people were continuously transported and every ship bound for the Caribbean contained up to 400 Irish people on average. The largest shipment once carried about 1,200 Irish people, most of them being single men. Shipments of Irish people, especially Tories and Catholic people, continued throughout the reign of Charles II until 1685. But the restoration of the Stuart monarchy gradually brought an end to large-scale transportations from Ireland.

Sir Charles Wheler estimated in his 1672 report that Irish Catholic people contained almost all the 800-1,000 men on Monserrat; the greater part of the 120 militiamen in the Leeward Quarter; most of the 60 in the English Quarter and two-thirds of the Kings two regiments on St. Christopher; at least half of the 200 men on Guadeloupe; and one-fifth of the 1,200 mustered on Nevis.[10] Consequently, the Irish were in the ascendancy in Montserrat by the end of the 17th century. According to a 1678 census, it had a community of almost 1,900 Irish men, women and children – a verifiable 50% of the population – existing as either indentured servants or freemen. Compared with the other Leeward Islands, it was 26% Irish on Antigua, 22% on Nevis and 10% on St Christopher. Because successive governors promised newcomers' religious tolerance and land ownership, servants from Ireland as well as Irish freemen from Barbados and other Leeward Islands flocked to Montserrat between 1660 and 1700. In 1655, the newly acquired Jamaica promptly became the leading Caribbean destination for Irish servants departing from Kinsale, Bristol, London and other Caribbean islands. In 1789, the Privy Council reported that there were 50,000 white people in the British West Indies and almost four-fifths of them were in the two islands – Jamaica about 23,000 and Barbados about 16,000. A major demographic change was that the British West Indian islands shifted between 1690 and 1710. During this period, slaves from Africa accounted for more than half the population on Antigua, Montserrat, Nevis and St Christopher and made up more than 80 percent of Barbados. Along with the increasing number of Africans, the Irish population started decreasing.

Another reason why it is impossible to count them is that the Irish came from all social backgrounds and they cannot be stereotyped. To make things more complex, not only did they hold various positions but those who were at the bottom of the social ladder often moved up, unlike African slaves who were not capable of moving beyond their status. Additionally, the Irish often changed sides in politics to take advantage of the situation. Some even willingly changed their religious beliefs to acquire land, status or spouse. Originally Catholic Irish people abroad were sometimes described in records as British or Anglican as they were technically always British subjects. For instance, there were the periods when no vessel was officially allowed to sail from Ireland directly to the Caribbean or elsewhere but by law, they were obliged first to visit an English port before clearance papers could be obtained. As a result, according to the official records, all Irish people who were on an Irish or English vessel arrived from England. According to law, the voyage didn't officially begin before the ship cleared from an English port, hence their origin could be described as British.

Girls and boys

According to the earliest state paper, the first order of the transportation of Irish children to the New World was on 6 September 1653: 'Order of the council of state. upon petition of David Selleck, of Boston, Geo Delle, master, and the Providence of London, Thos. Swanley, master, to pass to New England and Virginia, where they intend to carry 400 Irish children, directing a warrant to be granted, provided security is given to sail to Ireland, and within two months, to take in 400 Irish children, and transport them to those plantations'.

In 1655, the son of Oliver Cromwell, Henry, wrote to Secretary of State, John Thurlow, upon responding to a request from Jamaica for a thousand Irish girls and a thousand boys:

'Concerning the young women, although we must use force in taking them up, yet it is so much for their own good, and likely to be of so great advantage to the public...it is not in the least doubted that you may have such numbers of them as you see fit'. Cromwell recommended transporting between 1,500 and 2,000 boys of 12 to 14 years old, hoping to turn them English. The Council of State duly voted to transport 1,000 girls and the like number of boys under the age of 14 were to be sent to Jamaica with an allowance each not to exceed 20s. Girls and boys were often kidnapped by agents and soldiers while they were sleeping or snatched from the street. The man-catchers were paid 4 or 4 pounds 10s. by the ships' captains for every young woman or child.[11]

Some even estimate 'more than 100,000 young children, who were orphans or had been taken from their Catholic parents, were sent abroad into slavery in the West Indies, Virginia and New England, that they might thus lose their faith and all knowledge of their nationality, for in most instances even their names were changed'.[12] However, it turned out that young children were not actually very useful in the colonies. After some efforts to implement the scheme of transporting youngsters, the Council decided to focus on sending more mature men and women. Besides, this unethical kidnapping practice somewhat damaged the reputation of British colonies.

An anonymous poet wrote:

Tribeless, landless, nameless
Wealthless, hostless, farmeless,
Wander now thine aimless,
Children to and fro.[13]

Indentured servitude

Indentured servitude is an ancient system going back to the guilds of the Middle Ages. When the Ordinance of Labourers was passed in 1349, it began as serfdom. It declared that all men and women under sixty-year-old who didn't practice a craft must serve anyone requiring their labour. Indentured servants or apprentices had to sign a contract known as an 'indenture' binding them to serve a master for a few years. Between 1520 and 1630, the population of England more than doubled from 2.3 million to 4.8 million. As a result, poor and unemployed people became highly visible. The system of indentured servitude was a desperate attempt by the authorities to 'banish idleness'. Traditionally in England, an indenture or contract for labour, was used for farm labourers or apprentices who wanted to learn a trade. In those days, it was a perfectly common way to make a living and it contained no negative connotation.

The Virginia Company of London was created in 1606 by King James I with the purpose of establishing colonial settlements in North America. When England established the colony of Virginia, the indentured servitude system was widely introduced as a workforce in the New World mainly to work in the tobacco fields. Unavoidably, the system made people into chattel or property to be bought and sold during a certain amount of time. At the beginning, the company paid for transportation but it soon made planters and merchants responsible for it. In 1618, the Headright System began. This provided a grant of land, normally 50 acres to new settlers in the 13 colonies such as Virginia, Georgia, North Carolina, South Carolina and Maryland in order to attract more settlers to develop the region. A large number of newcomers, many of them Irish, arrived voluntarily by themselves and had paid about six pounds for transportation in the 1600s.

This system that Britain developed was applied throughout the British colonies. In the case of the British West Indies, instead of offering training opportunities, the master provided transportation, food, shelter and clothing during the term of the indenture. Prior to the 1640s, the majority of indentured servants were Irish, English and Scottish people who were willing to work in search of a better life.

Some of them who had capital and good contacts with England were allocated land and much of the land was quickly cleared to make way for tobacco and cotton plantations. Early servants typically received land at the end of their term, but soon there was not enough of it especially in Barbados, therefore they were paid a premium instead. The causes of leaving Ireland and the motives of the indentured workers were diverse. Early indentured servants typically signed a contract by which they agreed to certain conditions and for certain years. Adults typically served between four and seven years, while children worked for a longer period of time. In many cases, if indentured servants were 18 years old or older, the term of indentured service was shorter than for younger teenagers.

According to the correspondence of Malachy O'Queely, the archbishop of Tuam from 1631, two secular priests were transported to the Caribbean along with 600 people from Ireland. In 1636, a large group of Irish indentured servants were shipped from Kinsale to Barbados. The number of Irish Catholics in the British West Indies, mainly St Christopher and Montserrat, in 1639 were estimated to be more than 3,000 when the population of those regions was about 20,000. Then, Oliver Cromwell took control over Ireland. It was perfect timing for England as it was expanding its territories across the Caribbean and needed to populate and build the Empire.

To clear the island of Ireland, Cromwell captured as many Irish people as possible and transported them to newly acquired colonies. In 1654, the governors of some Irish counties had orders 'to arrest all wanderers, man and women, and such other Irish within their precincts as should not prove they had a settled course of industry as yielded a means of their own to maintain them, all such children as were in hospitals or workhouses, all prisoners, men and women, to be transported to the West

Indies'.[14] According to the state papers, incessant orders were issued during this period: 19 October 1654, Irish pirates and prisoners in Dorchester gaol, to be sent to Barbados, Bermuda or some other of the English plantations in America; 22 May 1656 to transport 1,200 men from Knockfergus in Ireland and Port Patrick in Scotland to Jamaica; 11 June 1660 the council of Barbados ordered field officers of every regiment to take an exact list of the Irish, and give an account of their number and place of abode and no Irish to be commander or sharer of any boat belonging to the island, among other orders. Destinations always seemed imprecise and unimportant.

Before the African slaves started arriving, it was Irish indentured servants who were the main labour force and the white population in the British West Indies. They were coming from all kinds of professions such as soldiers, prisoners, criminals, kidnapped children and grown-ups, vagabonds, priests, the men who refused to join foreign armies, the landlords who refused to transplant and whose properties had been confiscated by the Cromwell regime. Merchants and agents who recruited and kidnapped were often independent workers who made their own profits. In general, merchants were not able to make deals directly with servants in order to protect against theft by them. There was no political or legal legitimacy for their transportation. The practice of kidnapping was not uncommon as vagrants and criminals were caught across Ireland. A score of children, some of them as young as eight, were taken away or 'spirited away' at night. There was a skilful Irish agent who sold 850 Irish people in Barbados in a single year. The majority of servants were single men but quite often, whole families signed the indenture contract and moved to the Caribbean because agents gave false hope by painting a rosy picture of a great life in the tropics, good food and accommodation and the prospect of a plot of land when their indentures were completed.

As soon as England took Jamaica in 1655, it became a prime

destination for Irish people. The transportation of Catholic priests from Ireland systematically began, although priests had always been amongst indentured servants. Those in custody in Dublin but not found guilty of murder and those under the age of 40 were also transported there via Barbados. The condition of the Irish servants in Jamaica during the early years was similar to Barbados. According to the laws of Jamaica, there was the Act for Regulating Servants section, wherein the status of the indentured servants is described in detail: 'All servants shall have according to their contract and indenture, but where there is no contract, or indentured, servants under eighteen years of age at their arrival in this island shall serve seven years, and above eighteen years of age shall serve four years, and all convicted felons, for the time of their banishment; any man-servant marrying without the master's or mistress's consent, shall serve two years for such offence; all contracts made with servants or slaves to be utterly void; all suits between servants and their masters or mistresses relating to their freedom, shall be heard and determined by any two Justices of the Peace without any appeal; and if any servants absent themselves from their masters or mistresses service without leave, or a ticket from their master, mistress, or overseer, shall for each such days absence, serve one week, and so in proportion for a longer or shorter time, the whole punishment not to exceed three years'.

Irish people arrived directly and indirectly from Ireland. An agent Robert Southwell lamented people in Ireland in 1660: 'They have been so terrified with the ill practice of them to the Carib (sic) islands, where they were sold as slaves, that as yet they will hardly give credence to any other usage…' Some people, especially political prisoners, were transported around the world within the British Empire. According to writer Heaton Bowstead Robinson in the journals of the expedition along the coast of Africa, there was an incident in the autumn of 1825, near Cape Town: 'A short time before leaving the bay, about twenty people, natives of Ireland, came on board, to enter as seamen, who as we were short of hands were readily received; but almost immediately after they had got on board, a Mr, John Ingram claimed them from Captain Owen as his apprentices. In consequence of this application the Captain took them before the Commissioners of inquiry, when several deposed on oath, that they had been brought from their native country by force, some being afterwards persuaded to sign indentures, but others never having done so. Under these circumstances Captain Owen considered that they had a right to dispose of their own services; but Mr. Ingram obtained an order from Commodore Christian, desiring Captain Owen not to receive them on board, and a summons from the superintendent of police, requiring him to attend the Dutch court and submit to its judgment; to which he answered whilst we were under weigh, by protesting against its power to detain a British subject; but in accordance with the Commodore's order, the whole of the people were sent on shore, with the exception of one man, who contrived to secrete himself until we were at sea. The Captain wrote to Lord Charles H. Somerset respecting this Irish slave-trade, requesting him to see justice done to these unfortunate men, who born with all the advantages of freedom, were now suffering all the privations of slavery'.

Transporting convicts was not a British-specific system. The Spanish, the Portuguese, the French and the Dutch all did it. All those who were transported went through atrocious conditions and quite often this was virtually a death sentence as the mortality rate was extremely high. The system of indentured servitude was open to abuses on every side.

How they were recruited

According to various merchants' accounts, compared to their English, Scottish and Welsh counterparts, Irish people were more willing to work abroad because they were in extreme poverty. Being in Ireland meant there was no job prospects, no food and no hope. During the height of the servant trade, Irish ports and coast towns were packed with agents who worked for a fee for captains and merchants. For those voluntary workers, ship captains typically met prospective migrants at local inns, markets and fairs in Ireland. Advertisements were put in newspapers, too. For instance, an advertisement in the early 1770s looked like this: 'Capt. Woodside, will be in Ballymena on Saturday the 16th Inst. And the Saturday following, to agree with any passengers in that part of the country'.

Thomas Gookin was one of the most sought after and successful agents who made a fortune from the trade as he procured a large number of servants during the late 1660s and 1670s. In 1660, one merchant instructed his captain to sail to Kinsale 'to apply to Mr. Southwell and Thomas Gookin for servants'. In many cases, agents just picked up local people, gave no contracts and did no paperwork. For example, ship owner Matthew Cradock instructed Captain Thomas Anthony to get at least a hundred servants in Kinsale. Anthony arrived back in Kinsale on 28 April 1636 from the Caribbean but Dutch merchants had just filled their ship with servants for Barbados. It was not only British and Irish but Dutch merchants had also been engaged in the Irish servant trade by providing their own ships since the 1630s. Dutch merchants played a pivotal role in financing the voyage and supplying both Irish indentured servants and lucrative African slaves. To work efficiently in Ireland, they hired Irish agents. Those Dutch merchants were independent workers. Their names and ships were not registered with the Dutch East India Company (VOC) or the Chartered West India Company (WIC), so no records on their exact activities exist. According to some captains and agents accounts, Dutch merchants used ships of 100 to 450 tons to transport servants from Ireland to the Caribbean throughout the 17th century. The VOC officially owned 326 ships between 1620 and 1650. It is estimated that there were uncounted unofficial (unregistered) Dutch ships operating and Dutch merchants were trading all kinds of items and people. Just like Dutch merchants and ships were seen throughout the British Isles, Irish merchants and agents were also based in the Netherlands.

When a ship couldn't fill with passengers, agents were hired to kidnap children and lure grown-ups as quickly as possible in order to depart. On one occasion, Anthony was imprisoned when one of his agents kidnapped two local people, but he was released after a few days. There was a huge demand for tailors who provided clothes for the labouring population. A tailor Hugh Neal from Kinsale was hired to work in order to make crude garments at a cost of seven or eight shillings each for servants. After producing woollen and linen clothes, six dozen tin buttons, stockings and blankets, he received 18 pence per suit, eight pence per blanket, and 18 pence per dozen pairs of stockings.

By 1636, mainland American colonies such as Virginia had become less attractive because the wages were not high anymore. Irish people were adamant to go to the West Indian colonies as they knew they could make more money there. Quite often, early servants told the ship captain which island they wanted to go to. They were always well-informed about the conditions in the British West Indies and mainland American colonies. As a result, Thomas Anthony's ship for Virginia attracted only a few people. He had to change his destination for Barbados and quickly gathered several passengers. One of his reliable agents was called Thomas Belchard from Bandon. He was paid with a pint of wine for his work and some sugar for every servant procured. The *Abraham*, his ship of 150 tons, was finally filled and on arrival, the servants were sold within eight days and paid for at 500 lbs of tobacco each. The Barbados Governor picked the best ten servants.

Logistics of indentured servants

During the height of the servant trade, the treatment of Irish indentured servants was horrendous. The English governments referred to Irish people as rogues, vagabonds, rebels, neutrals, felons, military prisoners, bondsmen, slaves, amongst other derogative terms. They were shipped from every port in the British Isles but by far the greater number came from Kinsale, Cork, Dublin, Liverpool, Bristol and London. The merchants, both British and Irish, in Liverpool and Bristol always conducted trade with Ireland. Before crossing the Atlantic, English ships stopped at Kinsale which was the last stop to take on water, food and servants. The Irish were always part of this journey from its inception. The labouring poor of Munster who filled the ship were the earliest emigrants to travel through the Atlantic Ocean.

Prior to getting on a ship, some of them, especially those voluntary workers who were often young single men and women with no economic prospects at home, signed contracts which stipulated their length of service, while others were sold on the Barbados market upon arrival.

There were usually more male passengers but some shiploads clearly contained more women. For instance, in November 1655, a ship sailed out of Waterford carrying 19 women, 14 men, three priests and one married couple with their daughter. Some were the residents of Lackagh Castle. On one occasion, the authorities in Dublin ordered the removal of people because some were alleged to have been 'privy' to a murder in Kildare.

The New Geneva barracks and the Duncannon Fort in Waterford Harbour that are located on opposite sides of the estuary were used as so-called 'slave markets'. Before the Atlantic crossing, all passengers had a medical inspection in Cobh. At one time, there were three pregnant women and one with the French disease (syphilis) in the cargo. They were put ashore, while the pregnant women were given a shilling each and nothing for the one with the disease. By October 1636, Anthony filled the ship with 41 male and 20 female servants between 17 and 35 years old. The ship finally arrived in Barbados in January 1637. Eight people died during the voyage which was not uncommon. There were frequent outbreaks of disease during the voyage. Ten servants were sold to the Governor of the place for 450 lbs. All servants were sold within two days for 500 lbs of good tobacco. The ship was loaded with sugar and returned to London and then back to Kinsale again.

The passage to Barbados took between six and 10 weeks on average but it could be longer depending on winds and other factors. They had salted fish or beef, stale biscuits, milk, cheese and water but in general, food and water were poor quality and only a limited amount was available. The high mortality rate was the norm as there were always a few people who couldn't endure the voyage and died at sea. The ship was often packed like sardines and in some cases with 350 servants below deck. As a result, it was impossible to avoid spreading disease and infection. Sometimes, there were two or three dead bodies thrown away into the sea per day. It was not uncommon that only one-third of passengers were alive on arrival in Barbados, the first stop in the British West Indies. Passengers didn't only die at sea but often upon arrival as they were already quite weakened from the long sea voyage. Because many people didn't survive the journey or life in the tropics, the authorities focused on maintaining a constant flow of workers as it was detailed in the 1664 council report. The majority of those survivors never returned home.

Not only was there sickness and disease but some people were caught in a fight and died unnecessarily on board. Author of *Jamaican Partnership* (1839) Benjamin McMahon wrote: 'During our passage the most remarkable thing that occurred was the frequency of petty quarrels amongst the officers, which invariably led to a duel'.

Political prisoners were transported in a worse condition

than voluntary indentured servants. Iron shackles were often attached to their neck and legs. According to a witness' account: 'There was some sleeping, some spewing, some damning, some blasting and to make the scene odder, some were blasting father, mother, sister and brother...'[15]

Just like trading commodities, merchants profited directly from selling servants. Naturally, they always aimed at selling to the highest bidder. The merchant typically charged servants for the passage and the 2.5 percent commission when they were under contract to a specific planter. Indentured servants sold their labour in exchange for payment of their passage to the Caribbean.

The number of years they had to work varied depending on age and other factors but normally up to seven years on average. But in case of convicts or rebellious prisoners, it was not uncommon to serve for ten or more years. The prices varied depending on age, sex, professions, skills or sometimes even weight but merchants were generally able to sell their freight at prices 50 percent above cost of shipment. Around the mid-1630s, average prices were 6.10 to 7 pounds per person. In 1636, servants were sold for 500 pounds of tobacco each, which was probably approximately 12 pounds sterling in Barbados. For example, the average price in Maryland during the early 17th century was between 15 and 20 pounds and in Virginia as high as 40 to 60 pounds. According to historian Abbot Emerson Smith, in the mid-1650s, the average price in the West Indies increased to 10 and 14 pounds per person. One third of indentured servants were female who were 2 or 3 pounds cheaper than men. Skilled servants such as carpenters and masons were valued as they were sold for 25 or 30 pounds.

Payment for selling servants were typically made in colonial commodities or by bills of exchange. For example, it was a common method to pay in good quality sugar, cotton or tobacco in Barbados. When Thomas Anthony, a servant merchant from

Kinsale, sold a cargo of 53 servants in Barbados in 1637, he requested payment in good tobacco. Anthony gave three months credit to his clients as it was customary practiced in the trade. In order for rural planters to participate in transactions, the Barbados Assembly in 1635 ordered all merchants to wait at least 12 hours after arrival before starting sale. The most expensive item was the cost of food for servants during the voyage. The next highest expense was clothing. In 1659, one merchant supplied 100 servants to Barbados and incurred: victuals and provisions, 3 pounds per person (for a total of 300 pounds); clothes and blankets, 25 shillings per person (for a total of 125 pounds); for a total cost person of 4.5 pounds and for all one hundred servants a cost of 425 pounds.[16] In the mid-1650s, the indentured servants were sold for 1550 pounds of sugar per person on arrival in Barbados.

In 1670, Colonel Thomas Modyford, the first planter to become governor of Jamaica remarked that servant prices in Jamaica were almost the same as in Barbados. Modyford noted male servants in Jamaica were sold between 12 and 15 pounds, and females between 10 and 12 pounds in 1670. Towards the end of the 17th century, servant prices dramatically increased in spite of steady shipping costs because white indentured servants became scarce. In Jamaica, a good tradesman was about 40 pounds in 1739 and other less skillful servants went for 20 pounds each.

Freedom dues

The duration of normal adult servitude was around four years on average. Indentured servants typically received their freedom when their indentures expired. Upon emancipation from servitude, they became waged labourers by joining the militia or becoming overseers in the plantation. Depending on the region and the period of time, most of them were discharged with roughly 10 - 12 pounds sterling, or the equivalent in local currency, sugar or tobacco. It cost about 10 pounds to purchase a piece of land and plant tobacco which required only five acres for a living. Although, they had their freedom and money, by the 1650s most of the good land in Barbados and other Leeward Islands had been taken. No laws or regulations existed regarding freedom dues. Barbados and Nevis once had the most generous dues, a 10 pounds of payment, although it didn't last long. Here are some typical amounts:[17]

In Barbados
1630: 10 pounds
1647: land in Nevis or Antigua
1661: 400 lbs muscovado sugar

In Nevis
1672: 10 pounds
1675: 800 lbs of sugar
1681: 400 lbs of sugar
1701: 400 lbs of sugar or 2.10 pounds

In Antigua
1669: 400 lbs of sugar or tobacco

In St Christopher
1722: 4 pounds of money or 600 lbs of sugar

In Jamaica
1661: 400 lbs of sugar or 30 acres of land
1664: 2 pounds or 30 acres of land
1681: 2 pounds

Barbados offered five to 10 acres of land before the mid-1630s but the island was shortly filled and there was no more available land. The shortage of land occurred mainly because Cromwell transported an overwhelming number of indentured servants in a relatively short period of time. This changed the whole dynamics of the region and he ultimately changed the course of Irish and Caribbean history. As a result, the English authorities had to provide land for them elsewhere within the Leeward Islands or Jamaica after 1655. Because land was still available in St Christopher up to the 1680s, many former servants settled there and acquired small tracts of 10 or 12 acres.

Indenture completion

In the 1650s, a considerable number of Irish servants completed their indenture in Barbados and became free. But discrimination and other factors made it difficult to obtain jobs. Good land was already taken and it was too expensive to buy. Land was sold for 10 shillings per acre in the 1640s but it had become 5 pounds per acre by the early 1650s. The 500-acre plantation of Major Hilliard was valued at 400 pounds in the early 1640s which was sold for 7,000 pounds in 1647. The authorities in Barbados acknowledged that unemployed former servants posed serious problems or even a threat to the local community. According to the old minute books of Barbados, 20 percent of freed servants became farmers, overseers or artisans. But there is no record of what happened to the remaining 80 percent. Some probably left the island for other islands, joined the militia, become innkeepers, or shebeen owners (sellers of illegal liquor). Out of no choice, the rest of them were probably the ones described by Governor Daniel Searle as 'wandering vagabonds, moving constantly from plantation to plantation and inciting their compatriots to rebellion'.[18]

At the same time, the local authorities in Barbados rigorously believed that the Irish must remain at the bottom of society because of their 'Papish element' and tried to prevent the free people from obtaining their political rights which came with ownership of 10 or more acres of land. As a consequence, many of them had no means to hold good jobs and became waged labourers. Richard Ligon in 1657 observed the daily life of a plantation in Barbados where unskilled workers who made a daily wage of between 15 and 17 pence. Most of them got paid on a monthly basis. During the 1670s, when the slave competition became high, the wage level fell to between 4 and 5 pence. For obvious reasons, skilled people got paid better and found it easier to find jobs. Carpenters and masons received a daily wage of 6 to 8 shillings in the 1640s. Mechanics and artisans had been earning around the same wage by the 1680s.

When people became free, they moved to Bridgetown or Speightstown, the two largest port areas in search of work. They found work as porters and boatmen in the shipping and warehousing industries. But in many cases, people without skills remained on the same plantation working as waged labourers. For instance, Robert Frument worked on the plantation of Othoniell Higges in the 1670s. Because he was not able to secure a job when his indenture expired, he had to stay on the same estate doing field, manual and domestic work, and catching runaway servants and slaves. The Saint Michael Vestry in Barbados hired two free women called Ann Coleman and Tomasine Rayden as nurses and social workers at a monthly wage of 120 pounds of sugar. According to the Saint John Vestry in 1670, many freemen and poor whites in the parish drew their principal livelihood and subsistence by fishing after the local fishing industry tried to create more jobs.

But overall, freed Irish people often did well. An observer noted that 'ingenious and industrious men seldom failed to raise up their fortunes in any part of the West Indies'.[19] The ones with a skill climbed up the social ladder quicker. Richard Ligon, an English royalist who lost his fortune during the English Civil War, arrived on Barbados in 1647. Upon returning to England, he published a book called *A True and Exact History of the Island of Barbados*. According to him, Barbados needed 'Trades-men, as, Carpenters, Joyners, Masons, Smiths, Paviers, and Coopers'. Other occupations such as tailors, shoemakers, and weavers were also in huge demand in the colonies.

Becoming a land owner was the most crucial factor for Irish people. For those who couldn't own a piece of land, it was the main reason to leave Barbados. The authorities started encouraging them to settle in other British colonies where there was plenty of land available namely Jamaica, New England, Saint Lucia and Suriname, as well as French, Spanish and Dutch colonies during a certain period of time. According to some estimates, approximately 9,700 freemen and freeholders left Barbados between 1643 and 1662. About 1,600 people moved to Curacao, Grenada, Guadeloupe and Martinique; 800 people to Guiana; 3,000 to Saint Kitts; 1,300 to Saint Lucia; 2,400 to Suriname; 600 to Trinidad and Tobago. Planters and successful people tended to leave for the North American mainland colonies. A newly acquired colony Jamaica particularly provided favourable conditions for new settlers. Governor Lord Windsor tried to acquire more seasoned free people from Barbados by offering 30 acres of land and promised religious tolerance for Quakers and Irish Catholics. By the end of July 1662, he had persuaded King Charles II to order the Barbados Assembly to put advertisements in all parish churches.

Shift to sugar

At the beginning, England focused on growing tobacco, cotton, indigo and provisions. 1628 was the year of the tobacco boom and the indigo boom started in 1639. But stiff competition from the mainland American colonies depressed prices of cotton and tobacco. In the mid-17th century, the Dutch brought sugar cane from Brazil to Barbados. Sugar was a perfectly suitable crop for the Caribbean because sugar cane grew best in the tropical climate. The cultivation of sugar took off in the Caribbean where the English revolutionalised sugar production. England brought a vast number of slaves from Africa who eventually replaced Irish indentured servants. Local people were urged to change their main crops to sugar cane. Gradually, all British West Indian islands shifted to focus on sugar. The Caribbean soon turned into a labour intensive sugar-oriented slave economy.

Sugar did not bring slavery to the Caribbean as there were indentured servants already working in the fields but it certainly accelerated this shift. Unlike tobacco that could be grown by smallholders, sugar was extremely capital and labour intensive which required a large workforce of both non-skilled and skilled workers. The manufacture of sugar was a highly complex process. For example, skilled workers, mainly indentured servants, were often trained artisans such as carpenters, masons, potters and coopers who maintained the machinery of the mill and supervised the boiling and curing process. After the cane was harvested, it had to be crushed and boiled in order to extract the sugar. Unskilled workers planted, manured and weeded the crop. African slaves typically did manual work such as boiling and curing the sugar as the cane had to be crushed instantly to prevent its rotting. The mill and the boiling house were the most important parts of the operation. To extract the sugar crystals from the cane juice, instruments such as coolers, basins, ladles and cisterns were used in the boiling house. After boiling the juice to a certain temperature, the top part crystallises and the remaining liquor gets drawn off as molasses which could be distilled into rum. Slaves worked on scorching fields for hours and the boiling house was literally boiling hot and hotter than outside. They operated dangerous sugar machines and often got caught in the machine and maimed or/and killed.

Along with the rise of sugar production, other industries became highly sophisticated. The construction industry across the British West Indies, particularly in Barbados, started booming as the wealthy colonists and planters started building extravagant houses. Skilled artisans and workers were in huge demand particularly the ones who could 'draw a plan, and pursue the design they framed with great diligence'. For instance, a planter Christopher Jeaffreson in St Christopher was willing to pay good wages to skilled workers in 1681: 'for a tailor, a cooper, a carpenter, a joyner, a maison, a smith or such like – which are the trades most necessary here – I would allow to such one, when a good workman, 1,000 lbs or sugar wages for each year '. The sugar industry created an obvious hierarchy and a complex yet visible division of labour.

Shortly, sugar became the most treasured commodity of the British West Indies. England imported approximately 8,000 tons of sugar, mainly from Barbados in 1660 and exported about half of it. In 1770, Britain imported 23,500 tons of sugar and exported about 40 percent of this amount. The increasing consumption of sugar is related to the growing production of other tropical items such as coffee, tea and chocolate. By the early 18th century, coffeehouses had started mushrooming particularly in London and average people in the British Isles were increasingly enjoying those sweet colonial delicacies.

Barbados first shifted

Sugarcane cultivation in Barbados began in the early 1640s. Barbados was the first British West Indian island to smoothly shift to sugar and also to produce sugar for the European market. In order to cultivate sugar, a large labour force was necessary. The Dutch merchants provided sugar-making machinery and Africans from West Africa such as Sierra Leone, Guinea, Ghana and the Ivory Coast, Nigeria and Cameroon were shipped to work as slaves. The downside of sugar cultivation was that sugar canes took up the most part of the island and local food production became scarce. Barbados had increasingly become dependent upon imported provisions mainly from Ireland. The island received about 40 percent of salted meat from Ireland. Irish salted meat was hugely popular not just within the British

West Indies but amongst French and other colonies as well. Shorty, Irish provisions such as salted beef, pork, herrings and butter had become must-have staple food items in the Caribbean.

By 1660, most planters in Barbados had switched to sugar and the workforce shifted from indentured servants to African slaves. Initially, sugar was grown for the feeding of cattle and making of manure and fuel but in no time, it became the focus of the most important cash crop and commercial enterprise. As a result, by 1650, affluent planters had started becoming influential and only a few large landholders monopolised all the best sugar acreage. Early planters produced more sugar and profits as the yield per acre was much higher than later years. Sugar made the Barbados planters instantly rich. That's why, the term 'Barbadian planter' became synonymous with wealth and power. They were not just prosperous planters but also dominated the political scene. By 1652 in Barbados, there were 5,000 freeholders, 5,000 freed servants working for wages, 8,000 servants mainly Irish and Scottish and 20,000 African slaves. By 1700, the planters in Barbados, Jamaica and the Leeward Islands supplied nearly half the sugar consumed in Western Europe.

Unlike Barbados, other islands were slow to shift to sugar. Apart from having fertile soil and being geographically suitable for agriculture, there are some factors that made Barbados the greatest sugar producer. The islands such as St Christopher, Nevis and Montserrat have a rugged and mountainous terrain and clearing land for plantations was not straightforward. All British West Indian islands had equal shares of natural disasters, such as hurricanes and earthquakes, but Barbados was relatively safe despite the fact that a couple of natural disasters damaged sugar crops, for example, the locust plague of 1663, a major hurricane in 1667, drought in 1668, excessive rain in 1669 and the great fire in Bridgetown of 1670. Also, colonists generally lacked access to creditors who were willing to help finance the development of sugar on those islands. Another reason was that at the end of the 1640s, tobacco and cotton prices recovered a little, which removed the incentive to shift to a new crop quickly. In addition, the success of Barbados was attributed to its unique location. It was geographically isolated and far from enemies, while other Leeward Islands were constantly attacked by the French, the Spanish, the Taino, the Arawak and the Carib. Political instability had influenced agricultural development. St Christopher changed hands seven times during the French wars, Montserrat and Antigua twice and Nevis once. The English planters were always afraid of 'rebellious papists', French and Spanish invasions. Irish Catholics didn't only inform the French and the Spanish of fortifications and military capability but physically attacked the English. Barbados Governor Edwyn Stede believed that the 'bloody Papists' Irish and African slaves who always aided the enemies would make Britain less powerful in the region. On top of being located amongst enemy territories, local factionalism between the Irish Catholics and English Protestants had a big impact on these islands. For instance, right after William of Orange invaded England in 1688, Jacobite Nathaniel Johnson and 130 armed Irish servants in St Christopher refused to accept his rule, but 'assembled suddenly and declared themselves for King James' and then proceeded to 'kill, burn and destroy all that belong to the Protestant interest' and moved on to the French section of the island. Such conflicts and fighting kept destroying plantations and crops, and as a result, slowed down the development of the sugar economy. With less obstacles, Barbados was able to promptly shift to a slave-based sugar plantation system, while other Leeward Islands were still growing tobacco, cotton and indigo until they finally shifted to sugar in the 1670s. Barbados dominated the Caribbean sugar industry until 1720 when Jamaica surpassed its production.

Jamaica shifted

With a little time-lag, the sugar industry in Jamaica and the Leeward Islands started competing within the British West Indies. When Jamaica was being developed as a colony, Sir Thomas Modyford who had nearly 20 years of experience as a sugar planter in Barbados arrived to use his knowledge and experience. He promoted agricultural settlements on Jamaica as deputy governor. He brought a thousand people, mainly poor whites from Barbados in 1664. Jamaica swiftly developed an intensive regime focused on sugar that complemented pastoral farming. Barbadian planters, servants and slaves brought their skills to Jamaica and taught how to grow tropical crops. By 1680, quite a few large planters had existed in Jamaica.

As the biggest island in the British West Indies, Jamaica had surpassed Barbados as the leading sugar colony by 1720. Jamaica firmly established a slave and sugar economy replacing Barbados as Britain's most valuable Caribbean colony. Although Barbados was perfectly suited for sugar, it couldn't compete with the size of Jamaica which is about 26 times larger than Barbados. Jamaica produced fine agricultural resources as there were plenty of rivers and mountain ranges crisscrossing the island. Jamaica is the only island in the British West Indies that has lushly tropical soils, with fairly constant temperatures throughout the year. Eventually, piracy replaced sugar as Jamaica's main source of income as the production of Jamaican sugar started decreasing and became less competitive from around 1820.

Working conditions

On sugar plantations, servants and slaves both worked 10 hours a day from sunrise until sundown under the scorching heat. Their working hours were from 6 to 11 in the morning and from 1 to 6 in the afternoon. At large plantations, there was the ringing of a bell to signal the time to start working or finish off the day. They worked side by side cultivating, harvesting, processing sugarcane, raising livestock, fertilizing soil, growing provisional crops, maintaining plantation infrastructure, caregiving and other tasks.

Clothing

While African slaves were almost naked, Irish servants initially wore the same clothes in the tropics as if they were in Ireland. Irish servants eventually started wearing less clothing than labourers in Ireland but still wore more than the African slaves. Both male and female servants had to wear shoes and stockings to protect their feet against the chiggers. They had to deal with all kinds of insects such as ants and mosquitoes. During a certain period of time, a shirt and trousers (drawers) were the only garments for the majority of servants. They had no change of dirty shirts, some were in the fields even without shirts or shoes. If it rained and there were no spare clothes, they had nothing dry to wear to sleep. If they typically got cold and too weak in the morning, or they complained, they were beaten with a cane by the overseer. If they resisted, their time was doubled. Colonel Humphrey Walrond observed that servants were working under appalling conditions and believed that if their working conditions were better, productivity would be higher. He tried to improve their working environment by providing rug gowns to lie on and hammocks which was a privilege of the planter class when most of the time servants slept on wooden benches or on the ground.

They typically wore caps and coifs. Male servants commonly wore canvas doublets and breeches on top of smocks and skirts. For example, in Barbados, the male servants on plantations were provided with six shirts, one pair of trousers and three Monmouth caps in any given year. As for the female servants who worked in the fields, four smocks, three petticoats, and four caps were given. House servants were given an additional two smocks and three waistcoats per year. Many of them had to get a new pair of shoes every month because they wore them out so fast.

The wardrobe for 30 servants annually would cost 170 pounds, or 16 times the per capita expenditure for slaves' clothes. Basically the clothes of servants and slaves were made of the same material. Canvas was used to make petticoats for women and trousers for men. In the early 1650s, Richard Ligon outlined an ideal standard for servants' clothing. Men who were subordinate overseers annually should receive six shirts, two pairs of trousers, 12 pairs of canvas shoes, six pairs of stockings, three Monmouth caps, two canvas doublets (tight-fitting vests with attached underwear), and six Holland bands (hard-wearing linen garments). Male servants would need six shirts and pairs of drawers, 12 pairs of canvas shoes each year. Female domestic servants need six smocks, three petticoats, three waistcoats, six caps, and 12 pairs of shoes, while female common servants required four smocks, three petticoats, four caps and 12 pairs of shoes. Ligon also projected the costs and income for a 500-acre sugar plantation in 1650 could be about 8,866 pounds of profit and typical planters for this type of plantation were spending only 300 pounds for the cost of clothing and food for 100 slaves and 30 servants.

In Antigua, each servant had three pairs of shoes, three shirts, three pairs of drawers and one cap per annum in 1669. Barbados and Jamaica raised that by one pair of shoes in 1682, and the authorities promised to provide each male servant annually four shirts, three pairs of drawers, two jackets, one hat, four pairs of canvas shoes and also wages of 25 shillings per annum in 1696. Each servant had three canvas suits with hats and shoes each year in Nevis in 1701. In Jamaica, the clothing prescribed to be distributed annually consisted of three shirts, three pair of trousers, three pair of shoes, three pair of stockings, and one hat or cap and to the women proportionally.

Housing

During the early period, servants slept in hammocks just like planters, and slaves slept on the ground. But later, servants, essentially Cromwell's victims, and slaves had to find their own place to sleep as soon as they got off the ship. They slept separately but the way they lived was quite similar as they built their own huts or cabins from sticks, withys and plantain leaves. Typically, they both lived in small shacks with a dirt floor. Floors were dry ground and planks of wood were used as beds and furniture. In 1656, two servants complained that they had to sleep in 'sties worse than hogs'.[20] Servants' housing was basic and the structures had no value to be put in plantation inventories. According to a 1656 deed, a plantation included only a reference to '1 small house for servants to lye in'.[21]

Richard Ligon described a life of servants in Barbados: 'Upon the arrival of any ship...the Planters go aboard; and having bought such of them as they like, send them with a guide to his Plantation; and being come, commands them instantly to make their Cabins, which they not knowing them instantly to make their Cabins, which they not knowing how to do, are to be advised by other of their servants, that are their Seniors; but, if they be churlish, and will not show them, or if materials be wanting to make them Cabins, then they are to lye on the ground that night. These Cabins are to be made of sticks, withs, and Plantine leaves, under some little shade that may keep the rain off'.

To avoid insects and mosquitoes, they cleared the foliage around their houses, set smoky fires and daubed vinegar on the bites. Humidity, heavy rain falls and hurricanes regularly struck. Because Irish people were not used to the tropical climate, they were extremely vulnerable to tropical diseases and suffered serious mortality.

Food

Planters provided servants and slaves with food and clothing. In the middle of the 1640s, especially in Barbados, the rise of the sugar industry took up the majority of land and made it difficult to produce local food. As a result, local residents had to depend on imported food. Eventually, the cost of provisions rose along with the increasing population. The imported food such as salted meat and fish became the largest expense for planters. Because the staple food imported from Europe decayed rapidly in the tropical climate, meat products such as beef, pork and fish all needed to be heavily salted.

In general, slaves and servants ate similar food and they were constantly underfed. Their food was quite bland and monotonous. The main diet consisted of potatoes and boiled cornmeal. They sometimes ate pickled turtle. For Christmas, they ate slightly better meals such as poultry that had been raised by fellow workers. When cattle died, whether by disease or accident, servants and slaves received the dead animals. Servants would take the bodies of the animals while the slaves would eat the worst parts such as skins, entrails and head. If they complained, they were beaten by the overseer, and if they resisted, their time was doubled.

By the 1670s, skilled workers were able to eat fresh meat on a regular basis in the British West Indies. The wages of the common labourers reached 7 pence a day between 1662 and 1678 when pork, beef and mutton prices were between 5 and 8 pence per pound. In Barbados, the allowance of meat was fixed at 5 pounds in 1682 and in 1696 it was raised to 6 pounds. In order to reduce the level of malnutrition, a law in 1682 promised each servant and slave 5 pounds of meat or fish per week in Barbados. The labourer was able to complain at court if he didn't receive his pound of meat. When Jamaica was trying to attract more settlers, mainly by encouraging would-be indentured servants, it promised 3 ½ pounds of good meat or fish per week with sufficient plantation provisions, and it raised the allowance of meat to 4 pounds in 1677. The weekly rations in Jamaica were 4 pounds of good flesh, or 4 pounds of good fish, together with such convenient plantation provision, as may be sufficient. In Jamaica, there were plenty of food and drink although people were short of water. There were three daily markets which supplied plenty of cheap fresh fish, tortoise, pork, fowl, fruit and green vegetables. Locally grown beef and lamb were available albeit they were not up to English standards. Imported sweetmeats, sausages, oils, anchovies, capers, olives and other delicacies were also available. Native meats such as raccoons, rats and snakes were commonly eaten. As staples, they ate cassava, plantains, potatoes and yams.

Richard Ligon observed: 'their Suppers being a few Potatoes for meat, and water or Mobbie for drink. The next day they are rung out with a Bell to work, at six a clock in the morning...till the Bell ring again, which is at eleven a clock; and then they return and are set to dinner, either with a mess of Lob-lolly, Bonavist, or Potatoes. At one a clock, they are rung out again to the field, there to work till six, and then home again, to a supper of the same. And if it chance to rain, and wet them through, they have no shift, but must lye so all night'.

Drinks

In the late 1640s, as a by-product of the processing of sugar cane, rum became common on top of the ubiquitous mobby (or mobbie, made of potatoes) and perino (made of the cassava root). Rum or 'hot water' was a typical drink in the Caribbean and because of its easy availability, local people often drank it. As drinking rum was relatively affordable, many of them became addicted to it and it soon became one of the biggest concerns. Catholic priest Antoine Biet, remarked that drunkenness was great, especially among the lower classes and excessive drinking was a serious problem in all classes. Richard Ligon thought it was 'infinitely strong' and 'not very pleasant in taste'. Irish servants received a dole of rum and sugar for making punch on Saturday. According to Dr. Davy in 1864 writing about the physical and psychological state of the poor whites: 'Were white labourers temperate, I have little doubt they would be able to bear the climate of the West Indies infinitely better than they have hitherto done, and that they would have a greatly better chance of escaping most of the fatal diseases peculiar to the climate; and what is worse than bodily disease, that degeneration to which they are subject from the influence of intemperate habits and of climate combined – a degeneration of which there are too many and melancholy instances in this land, in the descendants of the original white colonists belonging to the class of labourers'.[22]

Local people in Jamaica often drank liquid chocolate in the morning. Hans Sloane, an Anglo-Irish physician and naturalist who visited several British West Indian islands, published a book upon returning back in London. While in Jamaica, he was offered a cup of local cocoa and water to drink but he found it 'nauseous and hard to digest'. Later, he tried to mix it with milk and sugar to make it more pleasant. A hot chocolate beverage – used as medicine at that time – brewed from shavings of freshly harvested cacao, boiled with milk and cinnamon was drunk by local people in Jamaica as far back as 1494. But Sloane got credit for inventing it because he brought this method back to London and a Soho grocer started selling it as a product.

Maltreatment of servants

The Irish Quaker abolitionist Ebenezer Shackleton compared the conditions endured by both Irish peasants and African slaves and concluded: 'In America the slave is called a slave – he is black, and is flogged: in Ireland he is called a labourer – he is white, and is only starved'. [23]

Because of their economic and social status, Irish indentured servants were constantly humiliated and treated atrociously.

Historians and researchers in this field have a general consensus they received a slave-like treatment albeit at different degrees. Anglo-Protestant prejudice gave all Irish people, especially Catholic people, an extremely difficult time both at home and abroad within the British system. Irish indentured servants, waged labourers, landless poor whites all rebelled against the ruling authorities. Maltreatment and discrimination of servants was the norm and extreme punishment and violence imposed on servants were daily occurrences. As a result, many of their lives got shortened.

In many ways, Irish servants were treated better than slaves and they were able to be free after a few years. But from a planter's point of view, they were not considered as useful assets during the limited short time period. Historian Hilary Beckles wrote: 'If we assume a seven-year average working span for slave labor and a six-year working span for servant labor, the slave, with an average purchase price of 30 pounds during the period 1635-60, had a man/year price of 4.2 pound; while the servant, with an average purchase price of 10 pounds, had a man/year price of 1.6 pounds. Using such simple economic calculations in conjunction with similar ones for maintenance cost, planters found servants a cheaper short term investment than slaves'.[24]

For example, a witness' account of Barbados in 1667 describes the indentured servants there as 'poor men, that are just permitted to live, and a great part Irish, derided by the Negroes, and branded with the epithet of white slaves'.[25] During their terms of service, they worked 'in the parching sun without shirt, shoe or stocking' – 'domineered over and used like dogs,' as Barbados' governor admitted in 1695 – and when they were free the scarcity of farmland and competition from slave labour condemned most to a wretched hand-to-mouth existence at the very bottom of West Indies society.[26]

Richard Ligon witnessed that servants had an extremely hard working schedule and received brutal treatment by overseers:

'Servants were typically called out by a bell at six in the morning and worked until eleven. They went back to the fields at one in the afternoon and remained there until six in the evening, returned to small huts made of sticks and plantain leaves'. He was appalled by the violence used to discipline servants: 'I have seen an overseer beat a servant with a cane about the head, till the blood has followed for a fault that is not worth the speaking of...truly, I have seen such cruelty there done to servants, as I did not think on Christian could have done to another'. And whether a master was merciful of cruel it shaped the experience of individual servants: 'Those that are merciful, treat their Servants well, both in their meat, drink, and lodging, and give them such work as is not unfit for Christians to do. But if the Masters be cruel, the Servants have very wearisome and miserable lives'.

In 1656, a servant Patrick Miller charged his master James Cornelius for beating him to the point that he was 'uncapable of doing him any service'. Francis Leaver and his brother-in-law Samuel Hodgskins hanged Leaver's servant John Thomas 'by the handes' and put 'fire matches betweene his fingers' which costed the servant 'the use of severall joynts (sic)'. The Barbados Council in 1661 acknowledged that some masters 'have exercised violence and great oppression, to, and upon their Servants, through which some of them have been murdered and destroyed'.

Antoine Biet, a French Catholic priest arrived in Barbados in 1654 and stayed there for about 3 months. He also witnessed how servants were receiving vicious treatments: 'All are very badly treated. When they work, the overseers are always close by with a stick with which they often prod them when they do not work as fast as is desired. I found it strange that they sent from England those persons who were suspected of being royalists and who had been taken prisoner (at the Battle of Worcester)... They were sold, especially when it was discovered that they were Catholics, the husband in one place, the wife in another, and the children in another place so as not to receive any solace from each other'.

According to Ligon, the most common method of punishment by masters and overseers was whipping. For example, an Irish man in Barbados received 12 lashes for swearing at dinner: 'if there was so much English blood in the tray as there was meat, he would eat it'. In a rare case, another Irish man called Patrick Cornelius was severely punished to the extent that he couldn't use his left leg and was no longer able to perform his duties. He petitioned the local justice in 1656 who admitted the punishment was far too excessive and freed him. Another Irish indentured servant Daniel Malisee talked scandalously about the planters of Barbados and in 1654, the Barbados governor in Council decided to put him naked in the pillory to endure the midday sun. When another Irish man spoke 'irreverently and profanely of the Holy Bible and other bad expressions of Englishmen' in 1678, the Barbados Assembly instructed the Provost Marshal to arrest and imprison him. Imprisonment normally followed a beating of the servant. According to another record on inhumane working and living conditions, in the mid-1650s: 'They now generally grinding at the mills and attending at the furnaces, or digging in the scorching island; having nothing to feed on (notwithstanding their hard labour) but potato roots, nor to drink, but water with such roots washed in it...being bought and sold still from one master to another, or attached as horses and beasts for the debts of their masters, being whipped at the whipping post (as rogues) for their masters pleasure, and sleeping in sties worse than hogs in England'.[27] In case of sickness, Ligon witnessed that they were likely to be beaten by the overseer and if they resisted, their period of indenture would be doubled. The extension of servitude was not uncommon and it was normally due to disorderly behaviour.

When looking at how the Irish lived in practical terms in those times in history, historians generally echo the finding of Barbadian historian Hilary Beckles that Irish indentured servants suffered the most intense day-to-day discrimination and humiliation in the British West Indies and their condition was 'nearer slavery than freedom'. According to historian Kerby Miller, 'They worked in the parching sun without shirt, shoe or stocking and domineered over and used like dogs and by the time they were freed they generally fell into a hand-to-mouth existence which consigned them to the very bottom of West Indian society'.

However, servants received some protection under the law. It was common practice for Barbadian planters to abandon servants who became unproductive as a result of sickness or disability. The overburdened poor-law authorities frequently complained that '...many masters, when their servants grow sick, and unable to perform their daily labour, will seem to remit some of their time to be clear of them, or turn them off to the intent they may not at all be chargeable to them for their recovery, whereby many of the said servants have most miserably perished'. To improve this situation, the code provided that a fine of 2,200 pounds of sugar was to be imposed on any master found guilty of wilfully abandoning such servants, to be payable into the parish vestry's poor law fund.[28]

Sluggish behaviour

The harsh life Irish servants had to endure made them not only rebellious but lethargic, showing passive behaviour. In 1676, Governor Atkins of Barbados complained that the servants who were transported to the island were useless: 'The most that come is from Ireland, and they grow weary of them for they prove commonly very idle and they do find by experience that they can keep three blacks who work better and cheaper than they can keep one white man'. As they were not being productive in the field at all, the governor wrote in 1688 that servants were unsuitable material for building colonial society: 'The most of the Christian servants of this island are brought out of the several gaols of England, Scotland and Ireland, or such whose lewd lives and conversations have taught them all manner of villainy, and reduced them to such miserable conditions of fortune that to prevent their starving they are forced to come servants to these colonies, where they cannot be maintained without work, many of which, having not been used to anything of that kind, will not set themselves to it, but run away from their masters, steal and purloin from them what they can'.[29]

It was not an unusual sight to see vagrants wandering about plantations and estates. In 1657, Barbados Governor Daniel Searle complained to the Barbados Assembly about the wandering Irish vagabonds refusing to labour: 'It hath been taken notice that several of the Irish nation, freemen and women, who have no certain place of residence and others of them do wander up and down from plantation to plantation, as vagabonds refusing to labour...and endeavouring by their example and persuasion to draw servants unto them of the said nation to the same...some are now fourth in rebellion, and refuse to come in, by all which it appears that could they be in a condition of power, or had opportunity, they would soon put some wicked and malicious design into execution'. Penalties were always given for those who harboured wandering servants or slaves.

In order to control these runaways and potential vagrants, Governor Searle introduced a pass system. All servants were issued a ticket so that masters or overseers would know whether they were travelling off their estates legitimately. If a servant was found without a pass, he or she was considered a runaway, arrested and whipped. Vagrants were considered as a potential threat as some of them eventually managed to escape to the French or Spanish colonies, while other joined the pirate fleets and roamed throughout the Caribbean. Particularly in Barbados, there was a persistent problem of Irish vagrants. Because there were simply too many Irish freemen and servants, the Barbados

Council in 1644 first and then in 1657 again ordered that any Irish person who arrived on a plantation and 'cannot give a read & good accompt (sic) of the reason of their coming should be severely punished'. But trying to stop them from arriving on the island by legislation proved to be ineffective as they were being unceasingly transported. Still authorities continued to petition against Irish servants, Governor Willoughby instructed the Privy Council to 'prevent any excess of Irish in future'. These regulations were apparently not practical and rather quickly withdrawn in the 1660s as there were simply too many Irish people to control, not to mention 12,000 military deportees, many of them the Irish who had arrived before 1655.

No weapons

In 1692, the authorities issued anti-Irish regulations which disarmed the Irish and forbid them to purchase weapons. Anyone selling arms and ammunition to the Irish or any Catholic people were punishable. What's more, their mobility was severely restricted and monitored. Not only an alliance of Irish servants and other non-Irish people but the collaboration amongst Irish servants, vagrants and landless whites were considered also a grave concern. The authorities knew what would happen when Irish people held arms. Planters constantly searched their houses to make sure they were not plotting something rebellious. Planters considered Irish servants as dangerous and constantly checked their activities. What they feared most was a full-fledged servant-slave alliance. In fact, the majority of them were former soldiers and knew how to handle arms. For instance, there was another uprising against British rule in Ireland, the Irish Rebellion of 1798, also known as the United Irishmen Rebellion. During this time, up to 30,000 were killed and a large number of former United Irish soldiers were transported to Jamaica. They were drafted into the regiments there but authorities lamented that as soon as they got arms into their hands, they deserted and fled into the mountains where they were typically joined by local maroons.

Irish oppressors

Although the large majority of the Irish were oppressed, quite a few of them were oppressors who were involved in the inhumane treatment of fellow Irish servants and enslaved Africans. When French priest Biet made his way across Barbados, he was befriended by an Irishman who was likely an overseer on a larger plantation. According to his description: 'He had in irons one of these poor Negroes who had stolen a pig. Every day, his hands in irons, the overseer had him whipped by the other Negroes until he was all covered with blood. The overseer, after having had him treated thus for seven or eight days, cut off one of his ears, had it roasted, and forced him to eat it'. The 1661 slave laws allowed any person in the colony (including Irish servants) to kill an enslaved African who was in the act of stealing. The killer would be rewarded with sugar and the owner would be compensated out of the public purse.

Rebellious Irish

Although they were the minority, highly competent Irish people in the ranks of British militia regiments controlled the rebellious Irish. Irish indentured servants didn't need to be rebellious or Catholic. Just being Irish could heighten tensions and was considered to be suspicious. Freed English, Welsh and Scottish former servants were always favoured. The most valued were Scottish who were viewed as hardworking, loyal and unproblematic. They became trusted allies of the English in the British West Indies and elsewhere. For example, Christopher Jeaffreson, a writer and planter on St Christopher wrote in 1677 that 'Scotchmen and Welchmen (sic) we esteem the best servants, and the Irish the worst, many of them being good for nothing but mischief'. The Irish servants were the most unpopular amongst planters and colonisers. In general, there was not a great demand for Irish workers. Catholicism has a lot to do with this infamous reputation. One assembly member in Barbados in 1667 remarked; 'We have more than a good many Irish amongst us, therefore I am for the downright Scott, who I am certain will fight without a crucifix about his neck'. Governor Dutton sent a message to London in 1683 to encourage more Scottish servants to transport and to keep the Irish at a minimum. As the Irish were not wanted, some colonies taxed or forbade them from arriving by using various means.

Irish people never stopped being rebellious because they were constantly mistreated and discriminated by the authorities, the judicial system, and were being imprisoned, killed and banished in Ireland, the British West Indies, or elsewhere within the British system. After all, it was as a result of rebellions in Ireland that Irish people were sent to the Caribbean. But the authorities kept mistreating Irish people and never improved the situation. It was a vicious circle. Anti-British rebellions by the Irish and resistance which included running away, arson, murder, revolt and passive behaviour continued. There is no shortage of court records and newspaper articles which reported the crimes committed by Irish servants. From trivial misdoings to grave offences, the Irish were involved with all sorts of incidents: an Irishman is a complaisant palavering fellow; Edward Coalman an Irishman is very talkative and much addicted to swearing... very positive in his answers; Daniel M'Inniry also an Irishman very apt to use the word really, talks very broken and backward and is fond of strong drink.[30]

Poorly treated Irish servants responded to atrocious masters by plotting rebellion. In rare cases, those people who were involved were executed, while typical punishments for attempted escapes included branding the letters FT on the servant's forehead or banishment. Irish people were always the primary cause of concern of English and Protestant officials.

They were considered as enemies within, more dangerous than African slaves who were considered more docile. By 1630, the authorities acknowledged that the Catholic Irish were a potential 'fifth column' for advancing their position in the Caribbean. One of the most suspicious behaviours of the Irish was the use of the Irish language. Just like in Ireland, English officials who had no clue about Gaelic considered it a secretive code, therefore they always thought the Irish were up to something. Even in the British West Indies, the authorities had this same issue and doubted the loyalty of Irish Catholics, and never trusted their behaviour.

As a result, master and Irish servant relationships were based on mutual distrust. Governor of Barbados William Willoughby also complained to his superiors in London that Barbados was 'in an ill condition, in regard of the multitude of negroes and Irish'. Moreover, the Governor in Jamaica Robert Hunter lamented the Irish are 'a lazy useless sort of people who come cheap and serve for deficiencies'. Generally speaking, plantation owners considered Irish servants and freemen as a 'potentially subversive lot' who had to be controlled and kept in a labouring status. They were Catholics, politically dangerous, refused to work and often ran away. The authorities and planters typically viewed them as a 'riotous and unruly lot' ready to overthrow the English whenever they had an opportunity.

Richard Ligon also mentioned the conspiracy in 1649: 'Their sufferings being grown to a great height, and their daily complainings to one another...being spread throughout the island; at the last, some amongst them, whose spirits were not able to endure such slavery, resolved to break through it, or dye in the act; and so conspired with some others...so that a day was appointed to fall upon their masters, and cut all their throats, and by that means, to make themselves not only freemen, but masters of the Island. And so closely was this plot carried, as no discovery was made, till the day before they were to put it in act: and then one of them, either by the failing of his courage, or some new obligation from the love of his master, revealed the long plotted conspiracy: and so by this timely advertisement, the masters were saved'.

In 1634, indentured servants in Barbados plotted to kill their masters and then take the first ship that came, planning to flee into the ocean as buccaneers. It was not the first rebellious act for the leaders, John and William Weston, as they had experienced the anti-enclosure riots during the 1620s and 1630s in Bristol, a major slave port in England. Another servant revolt in Barbados occurred in 1647 but this was a failed plot and ringleaders were caught and hanged. Another failed plot by servants occurred in 1649. They plotted 'to fall upon their masters, and cut all their throats and by that means make themselves not only freemen but masters of the island' but one servant betrayed his fellow conspirators and informed his master the day before the revolt. 18 servants were caught who were 'so haughty in their resolutions and so incorrigible' and executed for 'example to the rest'.

Countless Irish Catholics, such as James Jordan, Cork Farley, Daniell Hallsee, Anthony Clarke, Cornelius Bryan, Teage Dunnohan and Walter Welsh were accused of threatening the security of English people in Barbados. Cornelius Bryan received 21 lashes and was ordered to leave Barbados in 1656 for slander. Around the same time, two other Irishmen were flogged and put in a pillory for slander and mutiny. In 1657, Edmond Hollingsteade complained to the Barbados Council that his two Irish servants, George Dunohan and Walter Welsh 'have rebelliously and mutinously behaved themselves towards him their said master and mistress, whereby they have been in fear of their lives by the said servants'. Upon hearing the case, the Council ordered that 'the said Dunohan and Welsh received thirty-one lashes each, soundly laid on their bare back by the common hangman and returned to the common Gaol during ye pleasure of said master'.

According to some reports on Irish servants' misbehaviour towards their masters in 1657: 'Whereas it hath been taken notice that several of the Irish Nation, freemen and women, who have no certain place of residence, and others of them do wander up and down from plantation to plantation, as vagabonds, refusing to labour, or to put themselves into any service, but continuing in a dissolute, lewd, and slothful kind of life, put themselves on evil practices, as pilfering, thefts, robberies, and other felonious acts, for their subsistency, and endeavouring by their examples and persuasion to draw servants unto them of said Nation to the same kind of idle, witched courses, as complaints to that purpose hath daily made to appear; and information having been give, and oath made before myself and Council, that divers of, as well freemen as servants, have of late uttered threatening words, and menacing language, to several ye inhabitants of this place, and demeaned themselves in a very peremptory and insolent way of carriage and behaviour; and that some of them have endeavoured to secure themselves with arms; and others now forth in rebellion, and refuse to come in; by all which it appears, that could they be in a condition of power, or had opportunity, they would soon put some wicked and malicious design in execution'.[31]

Unlike Barbados, Jamaica never relied on servants. While plots by servants broke out in Barbados on a regular basis, in Jamaica, the initial threat of disorder came from soldiers and sailors that were mainly Irish and English. For example, soldiers who had not been paid staged a mutiny in 1661. Shortly, the army was disbanded and many of them received grants of land. Some stayed in Jamaica, while others joined foreign armies, took up piracy or moved to the North American mainland. Hugh Boyd McGuckian, a veteran of 1789 and former law agent of radical Arthur O'Connor, returned to Ireland and joined the 1803 Robert Emmet insurrection. McGuckian subsequently fled to Jamaica, where he joined the French army, as they tried to seize the island from the British with the help of local servants and slaves. Another United Irishman McClelland from County Antrim manipulated the blackballing and shunning of British regiment officers for their brutal treatment of Irish people in 1798 and sought refuge in Jamaica. One of the major rebellions by Irish soldiers in Jamaica was in 1795 when Irish regiments mutinied against their service in the British West Indies.

Jails

There were all sorts of offences that Irish people committed. During the early 1600s in Barbados, ordinary houses were rented by the authorities to confine law breakers. During Governor Philip Bell's administration between 1641 and 1650, a 'cage' was established in Bridgetown. Soon, another stronger cage was built to put some 'hundreds of seamen after a grave riot'. The cage was furnished with stocks, pillory and whipping post. Initially, all arrested vagabonds and various kinds of offenders regardless of race were put into the cage which contained a number of Irish people until a new law in August 1688 specified that the cage was used for 'recaptured runaway African slaves'. In 1652, the government rented a house owned by Nathan Grasty which shortly became Captain John Webster's possession. But the wooden-structured house was not adequate to house these rebellious men. A seaman who was confined there threatened to burn down the place after he failed to break out. Colonel Richard Hawkins was responsible for rebuilding the Webster's old deteriorating house. The first official common jail, or 'a sufficient mastic-frame house' in Bridgetown was re-built in 1655 costing some 6,117 pounds of sugar. By the 1690s, many Irish people were put in various unspecified prisons in Barbados, allegedly giving the French intelligence about the fortifications and strength of the island.

Alliance with Catholic enemies

Colonial officials and planters constantly feared that the Irish were plotting insurrection with foreign enemies and making allegiances with Catholics from rival empires such as France and Spain. As a matter of fact, the Irish would constantly align themselves with them. For example, Irish servants on Nevis cried of 'liberty' when Spanish forces started invading the island in 1629. When England tried to take over Hispaniola from Spain in 1655, Irish Catholics led English forces into a trap by pretending to be loyal to the English troops.

Irish servants rose up in St Christopher in 1666 and 1668, and in Montserrat in 1667, and defected to the invading French forces. In Antigua and Montserrat, the British repeatedly arrested and deported pro-French Irish servants.

When England entered the war against France and the Netherlands for the West Indian possessions in 1666, nearly 500 Irish indentured servants in Montserrat pledged their allegiance to the Catholic Louis XIV and aided France. In 1668, angry and dispossessed planters signed a petition against the rebellious Irish to Lord Willoughby of Parham, captain general of Barbados and the British Leeward Islands. 27 people in Montserrat signed the petition and most of them were Irish people. Amongst them was David Galway from Ireland who came to Montserrat in the 1660s. As he arrived with capital, he instantly acquired offices and a plantation in the parish of St. Patrick. It contained 1,300 acres of land and had all the machinery for sugar production, such as a boiling house, a cattle mill, a windmill and an assemblage of stair-stepped cisterns and 74 African slaves and Irish indentured servants. In 1669, Galway was strategically appointed to be in charge of law enforcement by Governor Willoughby in the south western region of Montserrat where most of the population were underprivileged Irish people. By the mid-1670s, he had become a major in the militia and a gubernatorial member.

St Christopher and Montserrat were colonised by both the

French and English in the 17th century. One of the most damaging conflicts was when French troops and rebellious Irish servants ravaged St Christopher, Montserrat and Antigua from 1666 to 1667. The conflict burned homes, crops and settlements across the islands. In 1688, Irish Catholics were accused of being part of a Catholic conspiracy in Barbados. James Hanley, the Irish sugar boiler on Jacob English's plantation allegedly suggested to English servants that if the French attacked Barbados, the Irish would 'quickly make way for the French to come in'. Christopher Codrington senior, the governor of Barbados and the Leeward Islands, tried to prevent uprisings in the Leeward Islands between 1689 and 1690 by shipping suspected Irish leaders and those who were willing to turn the British colonies over to the French and others. When the lieutenant governor of Montserrat Colonel Nathaniel Blakiston, a Catholic loyal to the English crown, learned that the Irish were plotting something for the French, he wrote to Codrington and asked for advice whether he should banish prominent Irish leaders or confiscate their lands.

In 1694, Governor William Beeston in Jamaica suspected that Irish Papists were encouraging the French to invade the islands. The Jamaica Assembly passed an act 'to prevent dangers that may arise from disguised as well as declared Papists' in 1729. This responded to public statements by Irish servants that 'they would not fight the Spaniards in the event that they attacked Jamaica, and to their alleged secret correspondence with the Spaniards in Cuba'.

Alliance with slaves

The co-operation between servants and slaves was another great concern for the authorities and planters. Irish people often joined with African slaves in plots of revolt and sea escapes.

The first recorded rebellious alliance in the Caribbean was in the winter of 1655. The Barbados Council recorded for the first time when Captain Richard Goodall and John Jones informed them: 'There were several Irish servants and negroes out in Rebellion in the Thicketts & thereabouts'. The Thicketts was a heavily wooded area in the south eastern regions of St Philip Parish. It was during the time when sugar plantation culture had not yet been well-established, they rebelled, killed plantation owners and destroyed crops. Governor Searle ordered that they 'be destroyed' by the local militia which consisted of mainly Irish freemen and servants: 'Lt. Col. Higginbottom (or Higginbotham) ...to raise any of the companies of Col. Henry Hawley's regiment, to follow ye said servants and runaway negroes, and if he shall meet with any of them, to cause them forthwith to be secured, and send them before the Governor, or some Justice of the Peace. But if the said servants and runaway negroes shall make any opposition, and resist his forces, and refuse to come in peaceably and submit themselves, then to use his utmost endeavours to suppress or destroy them, providing they do stand out in rebellion, and cannot be taken otherwise'. It took the authorities approximately two years to suppress the disorder.

On a smaller scale, various plots of rebellious alliance frequently occurred but there were some major ones in 1675, 1686 and 1692 in Barbados. To stabilise the situation, the authorities in Barbados tried to separate the servants, slaves and religious radicals from each other. But it didn't work. When another conspiracy of slaves and Irish servants was recorded in 1692, the objectives of the conspiracy were: to kill the governor, liberate certain slaves from the prisons, take the fort, seize the arms and take control of Barbados. They employed six Irishmen for their 'grand strategy for obtaining possession of the fort and arms'. Bridgetown was to be burned down and the 'most trusted slaves' planned to kill their masters while they slept at night. But the plot was betrayed at the last moment. This was the last rebellious alliance planned by servants and slaves in Barbados.

Slaves get heavier punishment

Although the servants and slaves both participated and played the same role, they received different punishments when they were caught. On a regular basis, planters informed the Assembly of Barbados that runaway servants and slaves had burned the canes as revenge on their masters. Slaves convicted of such arsonist acts were typically executed but a 1655 ruling of Council provided that 'if a servant or runaway should willingly burn or set on fire any sugar cane field, or other place where sugarcane is grown in any place in this island, shall for every such offence to be proved, receive 40 lashes upon his naked back, and branded on the forehead with a hot iron with the letter 'R' and become servant to the party or parties that shall be so damnified by the burning...for the term of seven years'.[32]

But in most cases, they didn't receive the same punishment. When another rebellion was plotted in Barbados in 1686, they were both caught. Irish servants were only imprisoned 'for being concerned, or privy to the late intended rising of the negroes to destroy all masters and mistresses'. According to John Oldmixon, an English historian, 'the Negroes' principal objectives in this revolt were to kill the masters, their wives to be kept for the chief of the conspirators, their children and white servants to be their slaves'. In the end, the Irish servants were freed, while 20 slaves were executed in a most excruciating way. The slaves were 'burned alive, drawn, quartered or had their heads placed on spikes as their bodies were reduced to ashes below', while Irish collaborators never received the same atrocious punishments that the slaves suffered. They typically received lashes and were sent to Jamaica or elsewhere. During another plot in 1687 in Barbados, the authorities caught Irish servants and African slaves. No servants were prosecuted, but 10 slaves were tortured and executed.

In Barbados, Lord Willoughby focused on keeping slaves in subjection in 1668 as the 4,000-strong militia contained 2,000 Irish

Catholics. While in Jamaica, there was a major rebellion from May to July in 1760 under an African slave called Tackay. Around 60 white servants and 400 Africans were killed. The expense of putting down the rebellion was estimated at approximately 100,000 pounds. In the Bahamas, rumours of collaborative plots by Irish servants and African slaves constantly circulated in the 1650s and 1660s.

Runaways

Indentured servants often ran away from serious hardships on plantations. The most common means was sea flight. Ordinances in St Christopher existed in order to punish anyone who sailed off with servants without authorisation. Those who successfully escaped normally ended up in Cuba, Puerto Rico and Hispaniola. They arrived on a regular basis from the British West Indies so the Spanish called them *Ingleses*, or English. Quite a few official records exist. For example, a group of Catholics, probably Irish indentured servants, from St Thomas, fled to Puerto Rico in 1657; 21-year-old Irish servant Joseph Marques escaped from the British Virgin Island in 1688; three fugitives sought shelter in Aguada, Puerto Rico in 1700; a former indentured servant with his African slave wife, 36 maroons and four Amerindian captives requested asylum in Puerto Rico in 1715; Diego Sky, an Irish servant from Jamaica fled to Puerto Rico in 1763; the authorities in Cuba reported Irish fugitives in 1768; to name a few.

In 1655, Admiral Penn and General Venables came to Barbados. They wanted to collect troops for their projected expedition to Hispaniola, and remarked that many recruits consisted of Irish who were 'a profligate race, who were in the habit of joining themselves to Runaway Slaves'.[33] Irish indentured servants were constantly running away especially in Jamaica where there were an alarming number of escapees in 1701. The Jamaica Assembly passed an Act 'to prevent freemen, white servants, negroes and other slaves running away from this island in shallops, boats and other vessels'. Governor Lord Archibald Hamilton in Jamaica reported that his counterpart in Santo Domingo sought to 'inveigle several Irish Papists settled in H.M. colonies...alleging it was for their interest to desert the tyranny these heretic dogs exercised over them'.[34]

Even though, the relationship with the Spanish was mutual as Irish runaways provided valuable information about British military conditions, Spain at times imposed laws that strictly forbade foreigners from settling or trading in Spanish America. In fact, some records show that Spain denied Irish people the right to settle in Hispaniola. They declared that for runaways or illegal foreigners on Spanish colonies to engage in commercial trade was strictly forbidden. For example, former Irish indentured servant Thomas Fitzgerald was deported out of Puerto Rico in 1770, and Daniel O'Flaherti was arrested and charged with smuggling goods. In many cases, however, the Spanish harboured runaway Irish servants and many Irish changed their names to Spanish ones, learned to speak Spanish and quickly integrated into their host societies.

Maroons

When the English defeated the Spanish in 1655, enslaved Africans on Jamaica ran away from their Spanish-owned plantations and masters to the island's interior, forming independent communities known as the Maroons. The word maroon comes from the Spanish word *cimarrones*, or mountaineers. By 1730, there were many second generation Maroons, or 'mulatto wenches' who were born in the woods. Mulatto was the term often used to mean any person with light brown skin or mixed race. The term maroon has been used to describe communities of runaway slaves in various parts of the Americas. The Jamaican Maroons eventually developed from settlements of escapees to flourishing communities. They even had their own political organisation and some of them owned slaves. They adapted themselves to the creole culture of the plantations and British ways of land use. Military policy and culture in general also influenced the Maroons. Irish people, especially the runaway servants, were living with them side by side.

Redlegs

Because the tropical sun burnt their fair-skinned legs, the term 'Redleg' is generally used to describe poor whites who laboured under the scorching sun in the British West Indies, but mostly in Barbados. This somewhat derogatory term was also applied to ex-servants, soldiers, underprivileged people and their descendants. It was not only physical appearance, but it also meant lower class. All Irish indentured servants were red legs in the tropics. But by the mid-18th century, their existence was unmistakably established in the slave society of Barbados and developed permanent social features quite distinct from that of the dominant white community. Other pejorative forms to describe the white underclass of Barbados include red shanks and eky-becky. Or backra as they were only permitted to sit in the back row at church. They often isolated themselves from mainstream society and economy.

In Barbados, there were several settlements where the majority of poor white people lived. For instance, Irish Town, is located in St Thomas near its border with St Andrew in Barbados. It is surrounded by the largest hills on the island. It was most likely established during the 17th century. An area below Hackleton's Cliff in the parish of St John had existed by 1650. According to an extract of the Journals of the Rev. Dr. Coke's Five Visits to America: 'There are more white inhabitants in Barbados than in the great Island of Jamaica, a considerable part of it being broke into very small estates of only a few acres, so that many of the whites are very poor, nay, some are even supported by the parish, a circumstance, I believe, not known in any other part of the Archipelago'.[35] Approximately, half of the white population of Barbados could be poor white and more than 50 percent of this group lived in extreme poverty. For example, in the returns for St. Peter, 94 poor white people were supported by the parish in 1780.[36] According to burial and baptism records from the parish of St. John, so-called poor white tenants were working as gardeners, distillers, labourers, shoemakers, masons, blacksmiths, carpenters, school masters, domestics, hucksters, and seamstresses.[37] When skilled African slaves started taking all kinds of jobs that were formally done by indentured servants, they were left out.

According to witnesses, they were visibly underprivileged. The son of an English soldier visited Barbados while his father was garrisoned in the 1820s and observed: 'Of all the classes of people who inhabit Bridgetown, the poor whites are the lowest and most degraded: residing in the meanest hovels, they pay no attention either to neatness in their dwellings or cleanliness in their persons, and they subsist too often, to their shame let it be spoken, on the kindness and charity of slaves, I have never seen a more sallow, dirty, ill-looking and unhappy race; the men lazy, the women disgusting, and the children neglected; all without any notion of principle, morality or religion; forming a melancholy picture of living misery, and a strong contrast with the general appearance of happiness depicted on the countenances of the free black, and coloured people, of the same class'.[38]

In many cases, they were hated by both masters and slaves. Although their standard of living was closer to the enslaved people than the average white population, being white, they functioned as a catalyst during the process of creolization. 'Used by the upper class as a buffer group against the enslaved population, the poor whites also acted as a filter for African culture on the island and, as such, were an extremely important agent in the creolization process. On the other hand, as the white group closest to the slaves, they were crucial to the diffusion of

European culture'.[39]

The poor white population gradually decreased as most of them passed away and left Barbados. But a few of them remained. After Emancipation, various attempts were introduced in order to improve their standards of living. Some of the early acts included the Ladies' Association for the Relief of the Indigent Poor and Infirm who started their Asylum and Daily Meal Dispensary in Bridgetown in 1825; a St. Michael's Clothing Club existed by 1838; 17 such organisations throughout the island existed by 1877; Daily Meal Societies were founded in St. Paul's district in 1840; and the Societies were operating in St. Stephen's by 1857; in St. Matthias by 1875; the Barbados General Hospital supported by voluntary contributions opened for the poor in 1844.[40]

Colonel John Scott who visited Barbados observed: 'Being poor men that are just permitted to live, and a very great part Irish, derided by the Negroes and branded with the epithet of white slaves'.[41] White people often wondered why free Africans and mulattoes on Barbados started thriving in many aspects by the 19th century, while the Redlegs remained at the bottom of the social hierarchy. Both wealthy white and black people somewhat looked down on them and they were regarded as objects of charity. Although they include many mixed race children, there are currently a few hundred Redlegs in Barbados.

In Saint Domingue, the term 'les Petits Blancs' traditionally refers to the poor, working class white population but in French colonies, the term could be also used to describe white people and it does not always contain negative connotations. Another term, 'black Irish' can also be used negatively depending on the context but when a British person uses it, it can often be a derogatory term. Generally, the term has been historically and customary applied to: the Vikings and Spanish descendants and immigrants with dark hair, dark eyes and skin in Ireland; the Protestant Planters in Ulster (by Catholics); Irish settlers and descendants of Irish who settled in the Caribbean; dark-skinned children of Irish and African origin as servants and slaves integrated; and to describe a regional ethnicity in Montserrat and Jamaica particularly when referred to a plot organised by servants and slaves.

Short life expectancy

Life expectancy in the British West Indies was extremely low. The majority of prospective servants were between 16 and 30 years old. The large majority of Irish men arrived at around 20, and the median age of death was 45, while it was 36 for women, according to a study of Jamaican and Barbadian tombstones for the years between 1650 and 1750 by Richard Dunn. Research conducted by Carl and Roberta Bridenbaugh also highlighted that at least half of the white population migrated to the West Indies by 1650 had died from disease, conflicts or overwork, in loneliness, misery and despair. For indentured servants, death was an everyday occurrence according to the Bridenbaughs. 'One third, possibly a half, of those between sixteen and twenty years of age did not live to attain freedom from servitude; and that between 1627 and 1647, more servants died in Barbados than emigrated from the island as free persons'.[42]

On a daily basis, servants were dying of tropical diseases as they were more susceptible to them. In Barbados, yellow fever was the principal killer of the people from Europe, while Africans were believed to have some immunity. Because it killed countless people in Barbados, the 1647 epidemic, in particular, it was called 'Barbados fever' or 'distemper'. Richard Ligon observed this atrocious epidemic stating the 'living were barely able to bury the dead'. A large number of corpses were thrown into the swamp adjacent to Carlisle Bay which contaminated water supply in Bridgetown. According to William Powrie's estimate in 1648, some 6,000 white residents, most of them servants, were killed. This obviously meant that long term plantation economy upon the use of white labour was not sustainable.[43] The fact that the servants from the British Isles were not reliable long term economic sources also contributed to the accelerated demand for African slaves during the 1650s.

Quakers

Quakers, or officially the Religious Society of Friends, was founded by an English man, George Fox in 1648 in Leicestershire, England. They were basically a Christian group forming their own organisation 'not quite the same as either Catholics or Protestants' and were advocates of democracy and equality. Their belief is that there is something of God in every person and that each human being is of unique worth. Quakers value all people equally and are particularly concerned with human rights and social justice. Fox's teaching, a new way of thinking and also a radical spirituality, rapidly spread across England and Ireland. Quakers focus on justice and simplicity and they don't practice sacraments and rituals such as baptism, conventional funerals and marriages. They became the most successful non-conformist sect of the 1650s.

The father of Quakerism in Ireland was William Edmundson (1627-1712). Born in Westmorland, England, he served as a trooper under Cromwell through the campaigns in England and Scotland. The first recorded official meeting for worship in Ireland took place in Lisburn in 1654. It was the Cromwellian soldiers stationed in Ireland that initially began converting to Quakerism or 'convincing' as they preferred to call it. Therefore, its roots in Ireland can be found amongst English soldiers, merchants and farmers who migrated after the English Civil War (1642-1651). Because the initial converts to Quakerism in Ireland were drawn almost exclusively from the English and Scottish Protestants, most of them had previously been members of other denominations such as the Baptists, Presbyterians or Anglicans. The majority of early Irish Quakers were of English origin, in other words, somewhat better off, who were soldiers, discharged soldiers, planters, tradesmen, artisans and farmers. Once the migration of those Quakers to Pennsylvania and elsewhere began, common Irish names, such as those starting with 'Mc', other Celtic prefixes or non old English names started to join Quakerism.

Major general of the forces in Ireland, Henry Cromwell, the son of Oliver, was intensely disturbed by his soldiers turning into Quakers and tried to crack down on the religion. He wrote to John Thurloe, a secretary to the council of state in Protectorate England and spymaster for Oliver Cromwell, on 6 January 1666: 'Our most considerable enemy in our view now are the Quakers, whoe begin to growe in some reputation in the country of Corke, their meetings being attended frequently by Col. Phaier, Major Wallis, and moste of the chief officers thereabouts. Some of our soldiers have ben perverted by them, and amongst the rest his highness's cornet to his own troop (Edward Cooke), is a professed Quaker, and hathe write to me in their style. Major Hodden, the governor of Kinsale is, I fear, goeing that way; he keeps one of them to preach to the souldiers. I think their principles and practises are not very consistent with civil government, much less with the discipline of an army. Some think them to have noe designe, but I am not of that opinion. Their counterfeited simplicitie (sic) renders them to me the more dangerous'.[44]

During the 1670s, livestock disease and crop failures in Munster caused chaos and a large number of Quaker families were affected. They 'had lived plentifully ...their Corn being spent and Cattle dead...shipped themselves ...to the West Indies to get food'.[45] In fact, there were various famines in Ireland which produced waves of Irish destitutes and vagabonds. For example, the famine of 1728-29, and then of 1740-41 which is known as *Bliain an Áir*, or the year of the slaughter, sent tens of thousands to their graves and thousands more to the New World. Wealthier Quakers in Ireland helped those victims, often referred to as St.

Patrick's vermin, by providing soup kitchens.

By 1750, there had been 150 Quaker meetings across Ireland. Regular meetings were held at Dublin, Derry, Cork, Waterford and Charleville, Wexford and Athlone. They founded the town of Mountmellick, Co. Laois in 1657. There were about 6,000 Quakers in 18th century Ireland. They shortly gained power and started being somewhat influential within Irish society. One of the most successful examples was the Quaker private boarding schools run by the Shackletons in Ballitore, Kildare. But they didn't become a prominent group in Ireland.

Just like Catholics and Presbyterians, Quakers also endured religious persecution in Ireland and they were imprisoned for their beliefs. Throughout the 18th century, many Quakers in Ireland fled persecution and immigrated to the Americas. Towards the end of the century, most of them left the group or converted to other religions.

When the transatlantic trade began, Quakers participated in all aspects of trade and investment. In 1650, Quakers started settling mainly on British West Indian islands and became planters, factors, ship owners, physicians and shopkeepers with the majority of them being merchants. Quakerism rapidly grew in the Caribbean.

Generally, they arrived with capital and education and would voluntarily work as skilled workers. There were approximately 3,000 Irish Friends who settled in North America and the Caribbean, especially in Barbados initially and Jamaica between 1682 and 1776.

Pacifism is one of their core beliefs which includes not only refusing to fight but to remove the causes of conflict and to bring peace. What Quakers strived for was social justice. In 1671, the founder George Fox came to Barbados and this sojourn had a huge influence on him as he faced the issue of chattel slavery on an island that completely depended on slave labour. He openly spoke against slaves' poor treatment while he was in the region. As the majority of Quakers were merchants, they were initially involved with servant and slave trade. But they started campaigning against slavery as the iniquity and injustice of slavery gradually grew and Quakers in Ireland, America and Europe showed a solid anti-slavery attitude. They were pioneer abolitionists. In 1688, Quakers in Germantown, Pennsylvania, issued the first public anti-slavery statement. North American Quakers began to expel anyone involved in slavery in the 1770s.

In most cases, Irish Quakers did well in the British West Indies as some of them acquired wealth relatively quickly because of religious freedom and the extensive merchant networks of the Society of Friends. Their influence was great at one point but short-lived except for in Jamaica and Cuba. Prior to mass migration to Pennsylvania, Barbados had more Quakers than any other English colonies. According to a report by Brett Brinegar, at the beginning of the 18th century, the numbers of Quakers were: 21,000 in Barbados; 9,500 in Jamaica; 2,800 in Antigua; 1,100 in Nevis. There is no breakdown for English and Irish Quakers. Just like the majority of Irish indentured servants, however, most of Quakers in the Caribbean had disappeared by abandoning Quakerism or leaving for mainland American colonies or elsewhere by 1750.

Quakers in Barbados

Since 1661, Quaker missionaries from England and Ireland often visited throughout the Caribbean. For example, Quaker missionaries Elizabeth Hooton and Joan Brocksop came to Barbados in 1661. George Rofe from England in 1661 described Barbados as 'the nursery of the (Quaker) truth'. Compared to early Quakers, those who arrived later were less persecuted in the Caribbean than early Quakers in Ireland, Britain or New England. They were allowed to worship freely as long as they paid their taxes and contributed to the cost of the military expenditures. Quakers in Barbados protested strongly against the colony's mandatory militia duty and actively evangelised the local slave population. Most early Quakers in Barbados owned slaves but at the same time, they tried to convert them in order to improve their working conditions.

While it didn't last long, at a certain time, Quakers in Barbados somewhat gained influence and power. According to a letter from William Edmundson, a travelling Quaker Minister in Barbados to Friends in Ireland in 1675: 'I have had good service for the Lord. Many are convinced and meetings so full that the meeting houses cannot contain the people. Many of the blacks are convinced and several confess to the Truth'.[46] By the 1680s, Quakers had five meeting houses and a couple of cemeteries, their own poor relief and own records of births, deaths and marriages, as well as their own physicians and midwives. Quaker merchants did very well especially in Bridgetown. The dramatic decline of Quakers occurred in the 1690s when there was a 'great sickness' on Barbados. It is believed that it was yellow fever and smallpox which claimed thousands of Quaker residents. By the 1690s, Quakers in Barbados were almost gone.

Quakers in Jamaica

Quakers initially arrived in Jamaica from Barbados in early 1658. Just like Barbados, quite a few Quaker missionaries from the British Isles also visited Jamaica. In 1671, George Fox visited the island and established seven meeting houses. Before the end of the 17th century, there were close to 10,000 Quakers in Jamaica. Their numbers had gradually trickled down by 1728 just like other British West Indian islands in a similar period. In 1837, English men Joseph Sturge and Thomas Harvey came to the British West Indian islands to help emancipate slavery.

The most well-known person who convinced many Irish people and others in the Caribbean was John 'the Quaker' Perrot. He was born in 1620 in Waterford and was a Baptist before he converted to Quakerism. He first went to Virginia, then to

Barbados where he spent some time and finally moved to Jamaica where he died in 1665. His views were often very independent and denied any form of organisation. He even refused to hold meetings for worship. Perrot was called 'hat heresy' because his followers objected to doffing their hats for prayer. Perrot was already an influential figure in Barbados when he moved to Jamaica. Governor of Jamaica Thomas Modyford was impressed with his 'good temper, skill and knowledge in merchant affairs'. Consequently, he appointed Perrot as a diplomat in Santo Domingo, the capital of Hispaniola. Upon completion, Modyford gave him land and a 300-ton vessel to transport between 300 and 400 indentured servants to Jamaica. Perrot made sure that the majority of them were Irish so that they became freemen upon arriving. But opinions about him were split down the middle. Although there is no doubt that his contribution was great, he didn't earn a great reputation amongst his fellow Friends. According to a Quaker's account: 'Largely, because the hat heretic emigrated to Barbados, and later to Jamaica, where clad in gaudy velvet and wearing a sword, he became a rich merchant and official, the worst furore subsided in England...Eventually however, retribution overtook John Perrot; he died heavily in debt'.[47] Another Quaker John Taylor described how: 'he lost his credit and repute among men and the very world spewed him out, and so he ended his days miserably and was buried in an old popish mass-house'.

Quakers in Nevis

A small congregation of Quakers had been established on Nevis by 1670. Because they refused to participate in Anglican services, they were resented by the local authorities. Two missionaries accompanied by a Quaker planter from Barbados arrived in 1671 but they were refused permission to remain on Nevis by the Governor. They were treated poorly and they had mostly disappeared by the end of the century.

Quakers in Montserrat

Joseph Sturge, an English Quaker, visited Barbados, Antigua, Montserrat, Dominica, Martinique, St Lucia and Jamaica. He made an extensive effort to free local slaves in Montserrat. As an abolitionist, he helped to establish the Peace Society. In 1857, he purchased the Elberton Sugar Estate to grow limes by free wage-earning labourers in order to prove that free labour was more productive.

The Sufferings of Quakers

Just like Catholics, Quakers were persecuted and discriminated against within the British system. They were also beaten and put in jail. Their sufferings were well-documented. Quaker Joseph Besse documented a couple of hundreds cases and published two volumes of *A Collection of the Sufferings of the People called Quakers*. Their sufferings were meticulously recorded from 1658 in Nevis, Barbados and Bermuda, Antigua and Jamaica since 1660. Meetings for sufferings were held on a regular basis and they took meeting minutes. According to the books, they were being punished for refusing to bear arms (serving in the militia), for not swearing oaths and for refusing to contribute to the maintenance of the priests. For example, John Jay in 1667 had taken from him one mare, for not fending to build forts, appraised at 3000 lb of sugar. Herbert Griffith in 1674 for not appearing in arms, 690lb and for priest's and church dues, so called 720 lb, in all 1410lb. In 1674, Roger Ellis, for refusing to fend into the militia, 3076 lb, for priest's wages, 102 lb and for refusing to swear, 2298 lb in all 5476 l. In 1674, John Taylor, shoemaker, for not appearing in Captain Robinson's troop, 2300 lb. These are just a few examples in the thousands of reported cases. Catholics and Quakers were often put in the same category. The earliest entry of the Quakers in the state papers was on 26 and 27 June 1660, 'Barbadoes (sic) minutes of the council of orders to be observed upon the approach of an enemy church wardens to take an exact list of all

Irish in their several parishes, and return the names of turbulent and dangerous spirits. Reasons against the being and sect of the Quakers within Barbadoes'.

Ulster Presbyterians

The Ulster Presbyterians, also called Scots-Irish, emigrated to the North American mainland where they became extremely influential particularly in Pennsylvania. In the mid-18th century, a large number of Presbyterians from Ireland started arriving in Jamaica and other Caribbean islands. Around the same time, Scottish Gaelic speaking highlanders who were exiled after the Jacobite rebellions and a series of uprisings (1688-1746) also pushed them out of Ireland and many ended up in Jamaica, along with Irish Jacobite prisoners. Ulster Presbyterians were present throughout the British West Indies. Some merchants and planters were described as: 'The Delapps from Donegal and Dublin moved in Antigua and Jamaica. The Blacks from Belfast in Grenada. The Gregs and Cunninghams in Dominica'.[48] Many of them worked as agents and overseers, sold Irish linen and provisions and handled slaves, but eventually emigrated to mainland America.

The Galway tribes

During the time of the Cromwellian regime, wealthy Gaelic and Anglo-Irish people also fell victim. Notable families from Ireland who lost their castles, land and all kinds of fortunes to the Cromwellian wars came to the Caribbean to regain lost wealth. Generally speaking, Irish people particularly with capital, skills and education who arrived as freemen all did very well in the Caribbean. With the profit they made, they typically repaid family debts, built Catholic churches and donated money to the poor back home. Some returned to Ireland or London, while the others remained in the Caribbean, emigrated to mainland America or elsewhere.

Unlike in Ireland, Catholics were less restricted in the Caribbean as they were able to hold office, buy or bequeath land. They got quickly involved with plantation industries, industrial, mercantile, and maritime enterprises that were linked to the plantation economies. As a result, the large majority of Irish indentured servants happened to work for Irish masters. In particular, merchant families from Galway, Kinsale and Waterford played a significant role in establishing their trading networks throughout the Caribbean, mainland America, France and Africa.

During the 1670s and 1680s, the Galway-based network of sugar-related business was firmly established. In many cases, the most visible families were from the Fourteen Tribes of Galway, powerful and prosperous merchant families who sent their sons (the second, third or fourth as the first son tended to remain in Ireland) to the Caribbean. Fourteen merchant families in Galway from the late 13th onward, dominated the political, commercial and social life in the city of Galway. They were the families of Athy, Blake, Bodkin, Browne, D'Arcy, Deane, fFont, fFrench, Joyce, Kirwan, Lynch, Martin, Morris and Skerritt. Except for the D'Arcy and Kirwan families who were of Irish origin, they were of Anglo-Norman descent. Some of their descendants such as the Lynches, Skerritts and fFrenches, established planting and mercantile dynasties until Catholic emancipation. They accumulated wealth by intermarrying into family members of the other Fourteen Tribes.

The fact that some Irish people maintained private or public adherence to the Church of Rome prevented them from acquiring political power in Britain and elsewhere within the British system. But in Montserrat, for example, religion was not the biggest obstacle and they were able to enter the ranks of local officeholders. Their focus was on solidly establishing themselves by consolidating the political, economic and social dominance of the planters and merchants, rather than helping underprivileged indentured servants.

The Blake brothers

When Cromwellian soldiers captured Galway in 1652, and expelled Catholics from the city, John Blake fitzNicholas's ancestral estate was confiscated. John had four sons: the eldest, Thomas, the second son, Henry and the third John (the same name as his father), and the fourth, Nicholas. To recoup their family's fortunes, John's three sons, Henry, John and Nicholas emigrated to the British West Indies in 1668, while as customary, the eldest son stayed at home. Upon arriving in Montserrat, Henry and Nicholas immediately purchased a plantation of between 500 and 1,000 acres in St. Anthony's parish. Henry managed their property until 1676 in Montserrat, while John worked as a merchant in Bridgetown, Barbados. Henry was doing great as a planter as he once wrote home to his brother: 'I am sorry you have very hard times, there is nothing sweeter than a good plentiful living, which, I thanke God, is not wanting unto your very loveing (sic) Brother'. As they all planned to return to Ireland after making a fortune, they left their wives and children back home. When enough capital was made, Nicholas moved back to Ireland in 1675 and Henry returned in 1676. By the time Henry returned home, he had possessed 38 slaves and accumulated enough wealth on Montserrat. Upon returning home, he bought a 600-acre property at Lehinch in County Mayo in 1678. Two years later, he also purchased an estate of at least 5,000 acres from the Earl of Westmeath at Renvyle, near Letterfrack, in County Galway.

Unlike his other brothers, John was not fortunate enough and struggled in Barbados. Believing that he couldn't make enough money to return home, John asked his wife to join him in Barbados. In May 1676, John purchased Henry's half of their plantation and decided to settle in Montserrat. As soon as he moved to Montserrat, John started prospering. In 1676, John was able to deliver the plantation and 'negers (sic)'to Edward Bodkin, his cousin, to whom John owed some money. Shortly, John became a member of the local oligarchy in Montserrat. According to the 1678 census, he was living on his Montserrat plantation and possessed 38 African slaves. By this time, he had become one of the largest slave owners on the island. When he died in Montserrat in 1692, he left 1,000 pounds and his plantation to his daughter, Catherine. She married Nicholas Lynch who owned sugar estates on St Christopher and Antigua. Blake & Lynch was one of the most successful sugar commission houses in the sugar trade in those days. In 1745, the family sold everything and emigrated to North America.

Ports in Ireland

Affluent trades made ports in Galway, Cork, Kinsale, Youghal and its surrounding regions develop rapidly. By the years between 1731 and the American Revolution (1765-1783), Cork, Dublin and Belfast had become predominant ports in Ireland. Galway was the first Irish port to play a major role in the Atlantic trade as Galway mercantile families established themselves in the Caribbean by the middle of 17th century. During this time, the port in Galway was briskly trading with Irish provisions and Caribbean molasses via Newport in Rhode Island. By the end of 1682, the port in Galway was a principal port in tobacco trade, landing approximately 10 percent of the annual import. In addition, it was Ireland's largest importer of indigo, most of which was landed directly from the plantations. The port in Galway also shipped substantial quantities of provisions such as salted beef, shoes and woollens.

Cork port

By the early 18th century, Youghal and Kinsale had started declining, and Cork had become the prominent provision port in the south of Ireland. Already Ireland's largest importer of tobacco and sugar between 1682 and 1685, Cork developed into the busiest port for provision items such as salted beef, pork, fish and butter. While the port's annual shipments of 16,960 barrels of beef represented about half of Ireland's plantation export of that item in 1686, Dublin's annual beef export averaged 5,590 barrels and 4,590 barrels in Galway during the same year. Irish merchants typically had contacts in London and mainland America and actively took initiative in the trade to the Caribbean up to the 1720s. Irish merchants in the Caribbean brought back a significant amount of sugar in London as they had great control over the supply of shipping space for the return voyage to London and American outports. For example, there were about 90 firms in London that operated as sugar factors between 1740 and 1775. Some of the notable Irish mercantile families in London were Arnold Nesbitt & Co., Andrew French & Co., and Blake & Lynch. Other merchants who were making large profits include William Gerrish, Peter Hussey and Nicholas Tuite. Naturally, they all had family members who owned plantations in the Caribbean.

Some of the high profile provisioning merchants in Cork between 1750 and the American Revolution were: William Delahoide; Benjamin Lawton; Francis Stacpole; Thomas Martin; William Winthrop; John Comerford and Archer & Patten; Richard Hare, Jasper Lucas, John Perry, Francis Gould; Laughton & Carlton. Savage French owned the *Snow Ann*, a 30-ton vessel which often brought rum, ginger, scrap pewter and iron from Jamaica to New York. Because the triangular trade had become widely common by the 1680s, it helped the city and its surrounding areas to develop. In 1700, Cork's population was 17,000 and it had grown to almost 60,000 by the end of the century.

Dublin port

Merchants in Dublin were also vigorously engaged in the

transatlantic trade by transporting a steady flow of indentured servants, slaves and provisions. By the 1730s, the focus of the trade had shifted to the middle colonies rather than the Caribbean and by the 1770s, Dublin had become Ireland's largest market for rum. In terms of the most Irish-owned ships registered, Derry's merchants owned 67 ships in 1771 and then Dublin had 28 ships around the similar period. Northern Irish merchants were known to be very efficient and often conducted their business with their own ships or formed a business partnership. Some of the prominent merchants from Dublin who traded in the Caribbean with their own ships were: Richard Grattan in the 1720s; Charles Anderson and Richard Walker in the 1730s; Samuel Lyons and Andrew Murray in the 1740s; William Delap in the 1750s; William Alexander in the 1760s and 1770s who shipped linens and Kilkenny marble for mantels and tabletops across the Atlantic.

Large companies were frequently engaged in lucrative triangular trading activities. Dublin partnered with a trading house Marsden & Benson from the mid-1740s. Marsden & Benson shipped linens to North America and brought back flaxseed, flour and wheat from North America, and sugar from the Caribbean which were transported to Dublin via Holyhead, Wales. Almost all firms run by Irish people in New York exported flaxseed and operated retail stores where they sold Irish, British and Caribbean items.

Kinship network

Just like they did elsewhere in the world, the Irish relied on their kinship networks in order to conduct business in the sugar industry and partake in the servant/slave economy. For instance, successful Galway merchants in the Caribbean all had family members in England, other European countries and the American mainland. Trustworthy family connections made it possible for them to conduct various credit arrangements for long- and intricate high-risk global trading business. Irish Catholic children of those merchants in the Caribbean were routinely sent to have Catholic educations in France, Belgium or elsewhere and to study something useful for trading professions, such as accounting.

There is no doubt that Irish merchants were able to smoothly conduct inter-island trade and global operations because of their extensive family networks. For instance, some of the most successful merchants who utilised their international connections in their trading business amongst Montserrat, England and Ireland include Robert Skerrett, Joseph Lynch, John Daly and Patrick Goold. Coming from a large mercantile family, a Cork man, Goold was a Montserrat representative for West Indias & Ginny Trade of Isaac Hobhouse & Co,. of Bristol in the early 1720s.

Irish Catholics in Ireland and abroad tended to marry Catholic people but mixed-religion marriages were not uncommon in the Caribbean. In order to maintain the kinship network and lucrative trading business, it was crucial to marry well. For example, Nicholas Tuites' three daughters all married high profile men. His eldest daughter married wealthy Thomas Selby of Middleton in Northumberland; another daughter married Thomas Stapleton, a member of the Irish merchant community in France; another daughter married Justin McCarthy from Tipperary who had a high ranking career in the French Army. For Irish merchants, this explains the kinship network was more important than religion. All the distinguished merchants in the Caribbean had extensive family contacts both sides of the Atlantic which was vital to conduct triangular trade. For example, Thomas Greer from Dungannon, County Tyrone, was a leading Quaker merchant who had family contacts with major Quaker firms in Philadelphia, such as Israel Pemberton and Coates & Reynell, and his chief customers for linen in Philadelphia were his cousins Samuel and John Morton. Northern Irish merchants were extensively involved with linen products along with provisions. On their return voyage, the ships that carried flaxseed from North America were typically owned by their relations, Irish firms or their branches in America. Caribbean items such as muscovado sugar, tobacco and rum that was primarily distilled in the North American mainland were bought by Irish merchants through their family networks. One of the main reasons why Irish people chose to be merchants was that it was relatively straightforward to make a living in commerce and trade because Catholic people were denied land ownership and professional careers in Ireland.

Trading

There is no doubt that the biggest export of Ireland was its people. Irish speaking destitute people in Munster were amongst the earliest people to cross the Atlantic and they were the greatest asset of the British Empire. Subsequently, Ireland established itself as a great provision exporting country. Long before the Atlantic trade started, Waterford fishermen and merchants had established trading routes with Newfoundland. When the servant and slave trade became prevalent, Waterford people essentially participated in the trade and started carrying provisions to the Caribbean where they were traded for rum and sugar for the Newfoundland market. They returned to Ireland with codfish from Newfoundland along with Caribbean items. Irish provision ports such as Galway, Cork, Kinsale and Youghal were already making a brisk business as early as the 1620s. English vessels stopped for the last time in the southern Irish port for water and food and loaded with provisions, textiles and Irish labourers before sailing to the Caribbean.

The Atlantic trade created a huge demand for Irish provisions which developed high quality food producing and packaging techniques. As a result, Irish provision industries had the most advanced meat curing and packing industry within the British system during the height of the Atlantic trade. Most notably, Irish salted meat products and rose butter were considered the most sought after food items as they were able to hold up in the tropical climate. Not only did Ireland produce high quality packed meat products but it also developed fine sugar-refining and flour-milling procedures for the European market and manufactured a wide variety of linen clothes and products for the labouring population that were a lifeline in the Caribbean.

When the slave trade became the norm, shipping operated in the triangular trade as vessels sailed through Europe, Africa and the Americas by using various shipping routes. Some ships stopped at the Canaries, Lisbon, Cadiz, Bilbao, Malaga or Madeira and traded provisions for wine, wool and other food items. In Malaga, there was a Waterford man Juan Murphy who was part of the high profile merchant class, while Irish settlements existed throughout the Andalusian ports namely those of the White, the Walsh, the Colgan, and the Fitzgerald's. Merchants constantly handled provisions, people and Caribbean items as offloaded ships needed to be filled before sailing to the next destination. Some people had their own ships and conducted their own provision commerce but in most cases, it was common to conduct a joint venture with the merchants in Bristol, Liverpool or elsewhere. Agents often worked in the secondary market and bought servants and slaves for their planter clients, while some people carried a small number of labourers and looked for buyers who were travelling from various localities.

Between 1678 and 1684, 290 ships returned to England from the British West Indies. According to their port of origin, almost half of these, 139 came from England, and the rest came from Irish ports. Quite a few American ships were dealing with Irish trade and merchants directly. The 40-ton brig *William & Susanna* of Salem, Massachusetts was one of the most active ships which sailed through the Caribbean, New England and Ireland. For example, the ship departed Salem in December 1713, traded

Caribbean items, calling at Guilford, Connecticut in February 1714. It loaded barrel staves and lumber, mainly bartered for rum and molasses and arrived in Cork in April 1714. There, the cargo was instantly sold and filled with indentured servants who were provided with all necessary items such as food, clothing and shoes. Other expenses namely the cost of handcuffs for the convicts and the wages of armed guards, were also charged against proceeds from the sale of the staves and lumber. In September 1714, the brig arrived back in Salem with 29 people and various Irish provisions.

Especially between 1670 and the 1720s, Ireland provided a vital source of colonial provisions. Until 1720, Ireland was the principal exporter of provisions to the British West Indies and remained as the largest supplier of salted beef and butter until the beginning of American Revolution in 1775. Throughout the 18th century, Irish beef primarily from the Cork region was the largest single import.

Compared to other European or North American products, made in Ireland food items were cheaper and better quality. According to some estimates, Ireland at one point provided more than half the food imported into the British West Indies. In terms of exports, the British West Indian colonies exported products worth 4 ½ million pounds annually to Britain between 1784 and 1786. During this period, Britain's domestic exports were in fact no larger than 14 million pounds. By 1763, sugar production in Montserrat and St Christopher was in decline, while Dominica, Grenada, St Vincent and Tobago started increasing.

Irish merchants carried all kinds of items legitimate or illegitimate. Most notably, they took part in the smuggling of tea to North America. A Philadelphia merchant wrote in the 1760s: 'Great quantities come here from Ireland and the West Indies'.[49] The provision ships carried tea directly from Ireland, brought sugar from the British West Indies, and returned to Ireland with flaxseed, flour and wheat. According to an Irish merchant in

Philadelphia in 1762: 'Tea, gin, brandy, silk handkerchief sell well here'.[50]

The Atlantic trade made Ireland financially prosper during this period. For example, Irish provision exports to the British West Indies increased eightfold between 1682 and 1773. Arthur Young, a writer from London, visited Ireland in 1776 and observed the Irish provision ports of Dublin, Cork, Waterford and Limerick which were economically growing with expanding infrastructure. Almost half the Irish exports to the British West Indies in 1792 consisted of barrelled beef, butter and port and two-fifths were linen-cloth and manufactured textiles.

Because the Caribbean demand for food and clothing items created various financial opportunities in Ireland, it started developing into England's rival country in overseas commerce. Britain even issued the Navigation Acts of 1660 which allowed Ireland to trade directly with the British West Indies. However, England soon realised that Ireland was making more profit, and promptly limited Irish trade activities by issuing the Act of 1663. As Irish provisions were paramount in the Caribbean, the law made sure that ships loaded with colonial items on the way back did not return directly to Irish ports, but via English ports. Ireland's vague status, as always, not exactly an equal English partner nor a completely subjugated colony, resulted in constant changes of navigation legislation.

Linen

As far back as 1000 BC, flax was grown in Ireland and linen clothing and its production is written in the Brehon Laws. During the Tudor times, linen garments were typically worn across the island of Ireland. Thomas Wentworth, the first Earl of Strafford was appointed Lord Deputy of Ireland in 1633. Along with him, the Duke of Ormonde encouraged the manufacturing of linen and a better quality of flaxseed was imported. In the late 17th and early 18th century, approximately 10,000 Huguenots, or French Calvinists, fled to Ireland. They were known as skilful artisans and traders. Amongst them was Louis Crommelin who settled in Lisburn, Northern Ireland and further stimulated the linen industry by introducing modern techniques. The linen trade played an enormous role in the social and economic development of the region. It was the linen industry that made Ulster thrive. It gradually grew and by the end of the 19th century, Belfast became the linen capital of the world.

By the 1760s, a large number of Belfast merchants were doing a brisk business in the linen and cotton industries. One of the most successful merchants was Valentine Jones who resided in Barbados. Because many Irish people tried to do business directly with the Caribbean, this caused the Irish free trade crises in 1778. There were three principal ports in England that grew along with the Atlantic trade. London was the leading slave port until 1698. By the 1730s, London had been replaced with Bristol. Then Liverpool overtook Bristol in the 1740s. Following the way Bristol and Liverpool prospered on the back of the slave trade, some wealthy Irish traders such as Waddell Cunningham hoped to make Belfast a booming slave trading port. The founding president of Belfast's Chamber of Commerce and an officer in the 18th century Irish Volunteers, Cunningham was believed to be the richest man in Belfast in those days as he made his fortune in slave trading. He had his own plantation in Dominica and named it Belfast. In 1786, he lobbied and drew a prospectus for 'a company of slave ship trading'. But he was met by strong protest from merchants in Belfast. The most prominent and vocal person against slavery was Thomas McCabe, a jeweller and member of the United Irishmen who claimed: 'May God wither the hand and consign the name to eternal infamy of the man who will sign that document'.[51] Throughout the Atlantic trade years, the majority of Belfast merchants remained rather modest and avoided openly getting involved with the slave trade, although the linen industry developed rapidly because of it. By 1763, at least 16 firms in Bristol and seven in Liverpool had been heavily involved with importing through wholesale linen merchants who specialised in Irish linen and other Irish provisions. By the end of the 18th century, linen accounted for half of Ireland's total exports but gradually started declining as cheaper cotton became widely available in mainland America and elsewhere.

Salted meat

During the Middle Ages, Ireland was already producing quality salted meat. Ireland had been pasturing cows for centuries. When England took over Ireland, they transformed much of the countryside into an extended grazing land to raise cattle for their own market. Local people were pushed off the best pasture and forced to farm smaller plots of marginal land. They started planting potatoes which was a crop that could be grown abundantly in less favourable soil. Eventually, cows took over much of Ireland, leaving the native population dependent on the potato for survival.

According to a state paper, one of the earliest orders of Irish beef as a provision to America was on 10 April 1633. During the height of the trade, Cork, Dublin and Belfast had world-class meat curing and packing industries. By 1668, the leading provision port, Cork had been producing half of Ireland's annual salted beef exports to various British colonies in the North American mainland and the Caribbean. Salted meat production started increasing and feeding the rising populations of the industrialised cities of Britain as well as slave populations in the Caribbean which made the impact of various famines in Ireland worse. Although, Ireland was a leading producer of beef, the majority of the local population were poor tenant farmers and their farms were owned by wealthy absentee landlords. They were able to consume only a little meat both fresh and salted. Beef was only eaten by certain privileged people in Ireland. Between the 17th century and the mid-19th century, most of the salted meat was exclusively produced for trade and exporting. The best and better parts of salted beef were typically saved for the British and shipped to England, British colonies, and the worst parts and lower grades were sent to non-British colonies, notably the French who were extremely keen on purchasing Irish meat. Because of its non-perishable nature, Irish salted meat was always the staple food of a vast number of soldiers across the globe who were serving the British Empire. After making huge profits, England was able to fund and accelerate the Industrial Revolution.

In fact, it was the English who started calling salted beef, 'corned beef' in the 17th century. The term 'corn' comes from an old English word which means large grain. 'Corned' refers to the large grains of rock salt for preserving the meat. Salt was mainly imported from Portugal and France and salted meat was produced from local cattle. Eventually local people in Cork started eating the salted beef to a certain degree and salted pork was more affordable in Ireland. Bacon and cabbage, a dish consisting of bacon or salted pork, potatoes and cabbage became a traditional meal in Ireland. Irish immigrants in America started eating corned beef instead of bacon which was more expensive there during the 19th century. As a result, this has become the ultimate Irish dish especially eaten on St. Patrick's Day. Although there were some Irish gatherings long before, the first recorded St. Patrick's Day parade and celebration was in New York City in 1762 accompanied by salted beef.

Post Office

Before the establishment of a post office, sea captains carried letters but those had to be duplicated because things tended to get lost at sea due to bad weather, pirate or enemy attacks. The General Post Office was established in England in 1660 and shortly throughout the British Empire in the Caribbean. In 1663, the Imperial Post Office established a Packet Agency in

Barbados. Jamaica also had a Packet Agency and an Irish man Daniel O'Neil was working there in 1663. But Jamaica was the first British West Indian colony to officially open a post office in 1671. Gabriel Martin was appointed to be the first Postmaster General of Jamaica and he immediately opened a post office in Spanish Town and then another post office at the port of Passage Fort in St Catherine.

Circular migration

Between 1660 and 1670, the number of indentured servants arriving in Barbados from the British Isles fell by 70 percent. At the same time, many of them in Barbados left for Jamaica, or other Leeward Islands, the North American mainland, namely South Carolina, Virginia and Maryland in search of land, opportunities and freedom. A small minority of people returned to Europe for good, while the others moved around within Caribbean islands, also known as island hoppers. They were befriended by kings and high-ranking officials of France, Spain and Denmark. For those who survived the initial ordeal when they first arrived in the Caribbean, the island they initially settled on was more like a stepping stone and it did not become their final destination. Irish priests also moved around although they were not spontaneous in most cases. An Irish Capuchin priest Father Maurice Whelan (1742-1806) was born in County Offaly. He joined the exiled Irish Capuchins in Bar-Sur-Aube, France, and served as a French navy chaplain during the American Revolutionary War in various places. After he was taken as a prisoner by Britain, he was transported to Jamaica. When he was released, he managed to get to New York and began ministering to fellow Catholic people. When Britain's latest acquisition, Jamaica, urgently needed to be settled, various attempts were made to attract settlers. Jamaica offered to pay the passages of emigrants from England in 1698, but it did not attract many migrants as England did not openly publish the act. Nevertheless, a large number of Irish Catholics came to Jamaica from Barbados and other Leeward Islands.

Political events in Ireland had a major impact on the lives of the Irish abroad. For example, Christopher Monck, the second Duke of Albermarle, was appointed Lieutenant Governor of Jamaica by the Catholic James II (1685-88) and his office was hugely supported by the Irish residents. But shortly, the Protestant William III took over and James II was exiled. When England declared war on France in May 1689, the majority of the Irish on St Christopher in the British territory crossed over the border into the French side, Saint-Christophe. France tried to destroy 'all that belongs to the Protestant interest' in St Christopher but this attack was a disaster as it caused the loss of many Irish defectors' lives. But whenever Irish people were persecuted or facing obstacles, there was always somewhere to go. The Caribbean Irish were highly mobile. When St Christopher's governor made an effort to get rid of disloyal Irish Catholic people from its island in the early 1630s, the Irish started settling on a neighbouring island, Montserrat. Another example is that the Irish always rebelled against the British and allied with the French, Spanish or other foreign powers. In 1667, the Irish plotted with the French so that they could beat the British and claim Montserrat and consequently France conquered the island. After this short French occupation period, many Irish planters fled to Jamaica and elsewhere and never returned.

Before England started transporting a quarter of a million people from Africa, there was a steady flow of Irish people to the British West Indian islands. Eventually, the growth of a slave-based economy diminished the role of Irish servants in the region. As the number of African slaves rose, the number of Irish servants declined. Former Irish indentured servants who were replaced by African slaves became small farmers or planters and gained more power and wealth. Between 1678 and 1713, Leeward sugar planters became extremely powerful and started controlling everything.

Previously mistreated Irish people always looked for greater freedom and a better climate elsewhere. There are no official records on Irish immigrants who departed from the British West Indies. Some official statistics are available but they are mostly the members of the Church of England. According to various estimates, approximately 12,000 left Barbados for other regions. Between 1678 and 1708, the Leeward Islands lost 30 percent of the white population. In 1667, an observer noted that most freemen who emigrated were tradesmen, 'worn out of their small settlement by greedy neighbours'. During the 1660s, other English colonies, such as New England, Saint Lucia and Suriname, launched campaigns to attract freemen from Barbados. These individuals, seasoned to the frontier, were highly valued. Their colonial experience in Barbados, in addition to their knowledge of plantation organisation, made them attractive as ideal labourers. Jamaica, the Leeward Islands, New England and to a lesser extent Virginia were successful in attracting these alienated freemen.[52]

Although most former Irish indentured servants often lacked sufficient skills to bargain for favourable treatment, those especially with capital, skills and education, often thrived in mainland America. For example, one of the most visible families who made a fortune in the Caribbean was the Bodkins who later established tobacco plantations in Maryland. Ultimately, the future of mainland colonies relied on the seasoned settlers from the Caribbean.

Moving up

A large majority of Irish people in the British West Indies started at the bottom of the hierarchy, but they ended up quite well off and had a comfortable life by the end of their lives. For example, by the 17th century, some 10 percent of Jamaica's landowners had been of Irish. An increasing number of average settlers like Teague Mackmarroe, who owned eight slaves, attained the rank of 'middling planter'. Once whipped for slandering, Cornelius Bryan's will reveals that after nearly 30 years in Barbados, he bequeathed a mansion house, 22 acres and 11 slaves with their increase to his wife Margaret and their six children. Irish settlers in Montserrat even became more financially and politically powerful than their British counterparts largely 'because they knew how to be hard and efficient slave masters'.[53] In some cases, Irish Catholics converted to Anglicanism to gain more positions of status, just as they had to elsewhere within the British system. This explains why many initially displaced Catholic people from Ireland eventually became active participants and an integral part of the British regime in the Caribbean.

On the other hand, some Irish people took advantage of the opportunity by taking their Catholicism in their stride as they escaped from servitude and defected to England's Catholic rivals. They joined Continental allies in religious colleges or military service, or moved freely through French and Spanish West Indian territories as merchants due to their loyalty to Catholic empires. The relationship was reciprocal. The Council of the Indies of the Spanish Empire often promoted Irish settlement in Spanish territories with land grants and monetary support. Many privateers and pirates in the Caribbean consisted of runaway Irish indentured people and a few of them obtained substantial wealth and status.

St. Patrick's Day

In 1766, James Grainger, a physician and poet in Nevis observed that the Roman Catholics were more privileged in Montserrat. In particular, the way they held their annual celebration on St. Patrick's Day. Because early Irish residents in Montserrat were planters and merchants before the huge influx of indentured servants arrived, they had established this annual Irish celebration at an early period compared to other islands. But on 17 March in 1768, when all planters were celebrating this annual festive day, the slaves tried to seize the festivities as they were left to their own devices. They thought the timing would be perfect for a rebellion during a St. Patrick's Day soirée at Government House in Plymouth. But a slave woman who heard some slave leaders talking about their plan informed her master and the uprising was halted. Several slaves were captured and hanged. As a result of this failed attempt and other rebellious incidents there was a restriction of civil, political and religious rights in Montserrat until 1798. The emancipation of slaves in 1802 restored civil rights but officially, the Catholic religion was still banned.

Religion

When openly Catholic James II ascended the throne in 1685, the lives of Catholics in the Caribbean significantly improved. Those wealthy Catholics started encouraging and promoting Catholicism. The Caribbean colonies adapted Catholic worship and appointed Catholics to higher positions. But his reign was rather short-lived, only lasting until 1688. In the British West Indies, some Irish Catholics were more flexible in terms of religion as they tended to embrace Protestantism more. Affluent Irish and Irish descent people often conformed to the Church of England, while many underprivileged Irish Catholics tended to hold on to their faith.

Those who converted were often buried in the Anglican churchyards of the parishes where they lived. For example, Nicholas Rice was a prosperous merchant who lived in St. Philip, Barbados. His nephew George Rice, owned a large plantation in the same parish. Both men originally came from Limerick and wrote a will. In 1677, Nicholas requested to leave to the Roman Catholic clergy of the city of Limerick 'where I was born one hundred and twenty pounds sterling'. In 1684, George requested to leave the poor of Limerick 50 sterling and the poor Irish people of St. Philip the sum of fourteen pounds sterling.[54] Martin French wrote a will in 1742 in Barbados and bequeathed an annuity of 10 pounds to the poor of the town of Galway, payable by his brother Andrew French. In 1750, Peter Blake in St Christopher left 200 pounds to his sister Mary in Dublin and 15 shillings to the poor of the parish of Knockmore.

William Stapleton from Tipperary was an Anglo-Irish landowner, deputy governor of Montserrat, and later became governor of the Leeward Islands. He is known for his successful governance mainly because he understood Irish people's needs. He allowed Irish Catholic people on Montserrat to practice their religion such as baptism and marriage. The Catholic Church often conducted the Irish-specific rites. For example, during baptism Irish parents tied 'a little peece of silver to the corner of the cloth wherein the chylde is wrapped while they also followed the Catholic practice of putting salt in the chyldes (sic) mouth as a way to purify the new member of the faith'.[55] Stapleton also acknowledged that some Irish Catholics in the Leeward Islands normally didn't have an issue with Anglican churches doing their paperwork for marriage licences and probate of wills. Moreover, Irish Catholics living in Ireland and abroad did not tend to marry outside their religion, but in the Caribbean, marriages between Protestant and Catholic Irish people were quite common.

For Irish Catholics, it was almost impossible without conforming to Protestantism to hold high positions in Ireland or other British colonies. But in the British West Indies, even though it was officially banned, Catholicism was not the biggest obstacle, and there were always ways for Irish people to purchase land for plantations and slaves to work for them and go into politics. In 1729, at least 20 percent of the assemblymen in Jamaica had Irish surnames. By the early 18th century, the families from Connacht and Munster, Archdeacons, the Kellys, the Bourkes, firmly had established a tradition of Irishmen holding the highest legal offices. Some of the substantial planter class people in Jamaica include O'Conner, O'Hara, Talbot, Coulthurst, Herbert, Gregory,

Martin, Madden, Forde, Richards, Dobbs, and de la Touche.

On the other hand, a large number of underprivileged Catholic people faithfully remained Catholic. Anthony Biet, a French Jesuit, who visited Barbados in 1654 wrote in his diary that an Irishman recognised him to be a priest and despite a lingual impasse spoke to him in the 'corrupt language' of Mediterranean sailors and 'almost fell to his knees in front of me, once again making the sign of the cross, and recited the Lord's Prayer in Latin, the Hail Mary, and Credo and the De Profundis to certify that he believed in the prayer for the dead, and he told me he was Catholic, Apostolic, and Roman'.

In 1666, an Irish Jesuit John Grace visited the British West Indies and spent three years travelling through the Caribbean. He reported to his superiors in 1669 that there were 12,000 Catholics in the eastern island of Barbados, with a total of 40,000 people, of which 8,000 were Irish Catholics and about 400 in St Christopher. Montserrat was entirely settled by 2,000 Irish people. There were 600 Irish on Nevis. In addition, a large number of Irish Catholics throughout the smaller islands including French territories were present. In 1702, Roman Catholic people were forbidden from settling in any of the Leeward Islands and this law was not repealed until 1753. This was specifically aimed at the Irish but it was impossible to implement.

There were already some Catholic people living in Jamaica prior to the take-over by England, as it was previously possessed by the Spanish but the only official priest was the chaplain of the captured French soldiers defeated off St. Lucia. Father Delany wrote in his book *History of the Catholic Church in Jamaica* that there were seven priests in Jamaica in 1684 and they had all come to the island as indentured servants. However, the bulk of the early Catholics were believed to have lost their faith within a generation or two. According to Edward Long, a British colonial administrator and the author of *The History of Jamaica,* the Jamaica Assembly held under the Governorship of the Duke of Albermarle who visited Jamaica in 1687 consisted primarily of Roman Catholics because of 'Father Thomas Churchill, a Romish priest who called himself pastor of his majesty's Catholic subjects in this island'. After Father Churchill left, there is a break of more than a century in the records of the Catholic Church in Jamaica. During this period, there were only occasional indentured servant priests serving the local Catholics. In 1730, the local authority imposed a 50 pounds fine on captains who imported servants from Ireland to Jamaica without knowing their religion. In 1791, the penal laws were finally abolished in England which meant Catholic people were allowed to have their rites and Mass celebrated legally. The authorities finally had to approve a Catholic priest. The Catholic bishop of London, Rev John Douglass was given the charge of finding priests for Catholic residents in Kingston. He sent Franciscan Fr. Anthony Quigly in 1792. By 1797 there had been some more Catholic priests on the island. Quigly remained in Jamaica until he died in 1799.

Persecuted priests

Ordinary people were transported to the Caribbean for no reason except their Catholic religion. And priests were not the exception. As a great number of Catholics were captured, the prisons across Ireland were running out of space. An order was issued in July 1654 that all priests in Dublin should be transported into Spain, but the destination was immediately changed to Barbados. Catholic priests were transported from Ireland as indentured servants. Ordinary Catholic people often harboured priests in Ireland and when they got caught, all of them were transported together to the Caribbean. Daniel Connery from Clare was sentenced to banishment in 1657 because he harboured a priest. He had a wife and 12 children but his wife died of illness and poverty. Three of his daughters were sent to Barbados and Colonel Henry Ingolsby wrote 'if they are alive, they are in miserable slavery'.

No legitimate reason was necessary to catch priests. They were not welcomed in the British West Indies either at all. In October 1654, when there was a murder in Lackagh, Galway, the whole population of 37 was sentenced to transportation and additionally a couple of priests were shipped to the Caribbean. In January 1655, when three Irish priests came ashore at Spike's Bay in Barbados, the Council was apprehensive. 16 months later, the Council banned four Irish priests from the island, giving them three days to leave Barbados. In 1656, 26 priests and Catholic schoolmasters from Carrickfergus were transported. In the same year, the Council learnt that ten priests had arrived in Barbados, and gave them 15 days to get out of 'the domains of the Commonwealth of England'. Because the priests were considered as a catalyst for the Irish population to rebel, they were often 'banished' (being transported without a specific destination or left adrift), rather than being sold or transported to a specific destination.

On top of forcefully transported priests, some of them arrived voluntarily as they were seriously concerned about the spiritual wellbeing of indentured servants. In 1638, the first missionaries of the Irish Catholics were sent to the British West Indies when Archbishop of Tuam Malachy Ó Caollaidhe (1630-1645), also known as Malachias O'Queely, sent two priests from his diocese, David O'Neill and Ferdinand Fareissy to accompany 600 Irish people to St Christopher where 'a great number of Irish live mixed with Scots and English'. O'Queely thought there would be great prospects of success for that mission because of the scarce presence of ministers but despite what was hoped, the two missionaries shortly passed away.

Father Stritch, an Irish priest from Limerick, arrived in the French part of bijurisdictional Saint-Christophe in 1650. According to Father Jean Baptiste du Tertre, a Jesuit, who witnessed Father Stritch's arrival, crowds of Irish were 'so fervent that they had no fear about exposing their bodies for the salvation of their souls'. Father Stritch founded a chapel in the French section and ministered to the Irish from the English part of the island for three months. He heard confessions and gave Holy Communion and baptised and instructed their children.

In Montserrat, priests secretly said Mass, or smuggled themselves from Saint-Christophe or other islands pretending to be indentured servants. Father Stritch also went in disguise to Montserrat as a timber merchant to offer Mass and sacraments to Irish indentured servants secretly practising in the woods for a while. Father Stritch shortly returned to Saint-Christophe but found the English had forbidden their servants to go to the French section. But many devout Catholics went there anyway although they were risking their lives. Consequently, the English captured 125 Catholics and shipped them to the desert island of Crabs and left them there. On another occasion, 300 Irish Catholics were captured in chains and shipped to this island.

In the British West Indies, priests were repeatedly imprisoned and banished. An Irish apostolic missionary Father Trinity arrived in St. Christopher in the mid-1600s. With other priests, he was put in a launch without food and water and sent to the Virgin Islands. It drifted, first stopped in St Thomas. They discovered local fruits such as bananas, oranges and guavas. Due to strong winds, the launch arrived in Puerto Rico where Father Trinity was put in the monastery by the Spanish. It wasn't until 1826, the British Assembly finally granted a Roman Catholic clergyman 100 pounds to 'furnish a convenient place of worship for his flock'.

Language

As English colonies, the lingua franca of the British West Indies was English. A substantial number of Irish people spoke Gaelic, while Africans spoke their own languages when they could. In a place where Gaelic speakers were the majority, all people picked up the language and accent as the slaves and servants constantly interacted and communicated. After all the populations integrated, this unique language was somewhat preserved. For instance, most residents on Montserrat at one point were Irish. Gaelic was believed to be clearly alive at least until the middle of the 19th century. Amhlaoibh Ó Súilleabháin (1780-1838), a diarist and Irish scholar found that Irish was still spoken in Montserrat by both African and Irish residents in 1831. He wrote on Black Irish: *'Is clos dom gurb i an Ghaeilge an teanga mharthartha san oilean sin Monserrat o aimsir Chromail, noch ar dibriodh iad. Cia dubh ban iad is gean liom cine Gael'*. (I hear that Irish is the native language of people in Montserrat, where the poor Irish were driven at the time of Cromwell. Whether they are black or white, I love the Irish speakers.)

In a letter by W.F. Butler in *The Athenaeum*, a retired sailor John O'Donovan, a native Gaelic speaker told a Cork civil servant: 'He frequently told me that in the year 1852, when mate of the brig Kaloolah, he went ashore on the island of Montserrat which was then out of the usual track of shipping. He said he was much surprised to hear the negroes actually talking Irish among themselves, and that he joined in the conversation'. Communication between the servants and slaves was not easy at the beginning but Creole English was quickly developed throughout the British West Indies. The development of Montserrat English and Jamaican English (Jamaican creole/ Patois) in general was believed to be strongly influenced by the Irish.

Entertainment

In Barbados, there were more white women than on any other British West Indian island at one point. Because it was a first call in the Caribbean after a long sea voyage, Barbados spontaneously developed all sorts of entertainment and sexual activities, such as gambling, cockfights, dances, tavern hopping and brothels. The most famous brothel owner was Rachel Pringle Polgreen

(1753-1791) who was born Rachel Lauder in Barbados to an enslaved African mother and a white master, William Lauder. She dropped her maiden name, when she got married to Thomas Pringle and then she added another surname after her second husband Polgreen. By marrying well, she accumulated wealth. She opened a tavern and the Royal Navy Hotel in Bridgetown during the 1770s. The hotel also offered sexual services to sailors in the British Royal Navy. When she died at the age of 48, she owned a considerable amount of property, such as buildings, liquid assets and slaves. J. W. Orderson, the proprietor of the Barbados Mercury, wrote a novel *Creoleana and the Fair Barbadian and Faithful Black,* first published in 1842. This earliest novel of this region is set in the Barbados of the 1790s, and its main characters include Rachel, Lauder, a Scot and a villain called Mac Flashby, an Irishman, who is described as a 'charming wild person' in the book. According to observers such as R. R. Madden, the boarding house in the British West Indies was 'something of a hospital as well as a restaurant and dance hall' as it had various functions. Quite often, mixed race women ran brothels.

Richard Ligon also witnessed that not just the white population but African slaves were also enjoying their day off when they could: 'On Sunday, they rest, and have the whole day at their pleasure; and the most of them use it as a day of rest and pleasure; but some of them who will make benefit of that days liberty, go where the mangrave trees grow, and gather the bark, of which they make ropes, which they truck away for other commodities, as shirts and drawers. In the afternoons on Sundays, they have their musick, which is of kettle drums, and those of several sizes; upon the smallest the belt musitian players, and the other come in as chorasses: the drum all men know, has but one tone; and therefore variety of tunes have little to do in this musick; and yet so strangely they varie their time, as 'tis a pleasure to the most curious ears, and it was to me one of the strangest noises that ever I heard made of one tone; and if they had the variety of tune, which gives the greater scope in musick, as they have of time they would do wonders in that art'.

In Jamaica, because Irish people and the Maroons lived closely, local folk dances that are associated with the Maroons are believed to be influenced by Irish reels.

Media

Because Irish people were mostly English speakers, they were always actively involved with the media industry as printers, editors and writers throughout the British colonies. *The Barbados Gazette* was the first local newspaper founded by London-born English man Samuel Keimer in 1731. Various journalists with Irish-surnames were working for him. He previously published *The Pennsylvania Gazette* in Philadelphia. Another newspaper *The Globe* was launched in Barbados in 1818 and the first editor was Michael Ryan. In Trinidad, M. Gallagher started *The Trinidad Weekly Courant*, the first English language newspaper in 1799. In 1825, the *Port-of-Spain Gazette* was established. While Spanish administrators tended to spread colonisation by using newspapers, the British considered it more as a commercial tool. *The Weekly Jamaica Courant* was established in 1718, *The Jamaica Gazette* in 1745 and the *Royal Gazette* in 1780 and *The Daily Gleaner* in 1834.

Inter-racial affairs

It was a common practice for the rich planters to have local mistresses because they often didn't bring their wives to the Caribbean. Due to a shortage of women, men with power were highly promiscuous. They didn't only sleep with their workers but some used their mixed-race daughters and granddaughters because they had only 'Negro and Maroon women to solace them',[56] as Henry Cromwell acknowledged. The Parliamentary Council knew it was a serious matter. Since the 1650s, the council constantly gave orders for the supply of 'loose wenches' to sugar planters in Barbados on a regular basis and also to increase the white population. When so-called 'loose women' were recruited from prisons and brothels throughout Ireland and England, local men were delighted.

Although it was not strictly enforced, throughout the British West Indies, a law existed that forbade marriages and sexual relations between white people and African slaves. Many who visited the region witnessed that there were quite a few light skinned slaves whose parents were obviously either a very fair-skinned European father or mother. It is also well-reported that female servants and slaves were used in satisfying the sexual demands of powerful people such as masters and colonisers, as well as ship crew who often raped and abused them during the long voyage.

From a master's point of view, a child being born cost money. It was not unusual that a master or servant fathered a child on a female servant. In Barbados, anyone who fathered a child on a female servant had to serve her master for an additional three years or provide a servant to do so, to compensate her master for the interruption of her work and the cost of maintaining the child. Male and female servants did similar work until the 1650s but the shortage of women made them particularly valuable sexual objects. According to the provisions of the 1652 laws, it 'priced' sexual relations with female servants out of the reach of male servants, and restricted access to female servants' bodies to their owners or other men.

Relations between Irish men and African women were also recorded and not uncommon. Richard Madden who was a special magistrate accidentally found out when he visited Jamaica that his uncle Garret Forde, a plantation owner, had a slave mistress and that he had several mixed-race cousins in Jamaica. Naval officer Charles Fitzgerald was 19-years-old when he wrote a letter to his mother in 1775 that 'the jet black ladies of Africa's burning sands have made me forget the unripened beauties of the north'. And he added: 'She could look forward to a copper coloured grandchild'. The shortage of women and the fact that many planters and merchants left their wives and family members back home also resulted in homosexual relationships and bigamists typically existed.

Mixed breeding

According to Sean O'Callaghan who found some records at the Public Archives of Barbados, long before the large influx of African slaves, white merchants were conducting a breeding business. Apparently, they saw a huge demand of prostitutes to cater the local white population. As early as 1638, they were buying the indentures of servant women and breeding from them. 'They were often the fathers of white children of such a union, and when the girls were old enough, at the age of twelve or thirteen, they were sold to the madams of the brothels in Bridgetown which were typically catered for the local planters and the ships' officers. When a girl had lost her looks, she was then resold to a lower class brothel catering for ordinary seamen, usually run by mulatto women'.[57]

The records at the Barbados Archives also reveal that these stud farms also specialised in mixed breeding. 'Coromantine and Mandingo men were usually chosen as sires, for among all the African tribes enslaved, they were considered to be the strongest and most intelligent. Careful records were kept, much like the ones they kept for their horses. A good breeder was an invaluable asset on such farms, but was often worn out by her early twenties, having had her first child at the age of twelve or thirteen. The progeny of such unions, particularly the females, were eagerly sought after by the local planters, who found the Irish sexually cold and unresponsive, having to be whipped into submission. The lightly coloured mulatto girls bred on the farms were, on the other hand, not only eager, but also trained for every kind of sexual proclivity. Many of them, therefore, fetched high prices in the brothels of Bridgetown, and some even ended up owning their own establishments. The mulatto boys were sold to homosexual planters or were given work as houseboys in the Big Houses'.[58]

Although no official or legal 'forced breeding' programme could be found, it is believed that female Irish servants were often forced to breed with enslaved African men. According to John Martin, a witness account: 'The settlers began to breed Irish women and girls with African men to produce slaves with a distinct complexion. These new mulatto slaves brought a higher price than Irish livestock and likewise, enabled the settlers to save money rather than purchase new African slaves. This practice of interbreeding Irish females with African men went on for several decades and was so widespread that in 1681 legislation was passed forbidding the practice of mating Irish slave women to African slave men for the purpose of producing slaves for sale'.[59] Apparently, some of the physically larger Africans were made to work as guards and overseers and were given certain privileges. Female Irish servants were raped by black overseers in order to produce stronger mulatto slaves who were more capable of working in the tropics. This practice was stopped only because it interfered with the profits of the Royal African Company. But just like slave breeding, the policy of promotion of servant breeding was not taken seriously. Nevertheless, the Assembly eventually imposed heavy penalties upon those people who made women pregnant by others and upheld the planters' right to extend the time of such woman servants by two years.

Soldiers

For a relatively small island, there are more than 30,000 castles and castle ruins dotted throughout the island of Ireland. A castle is a fortified building and used as a residence for military and defence purposes. It is where the lord, knight, king, queen or some powerful figure would reside. This is also the place where prisoners – who could often be noblemen and significant individuals – were kept. So this explains a lot. The Irish military tradition runs deep. Throughout history, Ireland constantly experienced wars and battles and had been fighting and producing soldiers for centuries. 'The Irish are a military people – strong, nimble and hardy, fond of adventure, irascible, brotherly and generous – they have all the qualities that tempt men to war and make them good soldiers,' wrote Thomas Davis, an Irish writer and politician who was the main organiser of the Young Ireland movement.

Just like clergy training, soldiering on the continent had been a traditionally established profession for Irish Catholics and gentry. Since medieval times, Irish mercenaries were in high demand in continental European countries. Because Irish soldiers were ubiquitously seen on the battlefields, their bravery was praised in all corners of the world. But it did not come without a cost. On the eve of the defeat during the battle of Kinsale in 1601 which was a war against English rule, the Gaelic Earl Hugh O'Neill remarked: 'We Irishmen are exiled and made bond-slaves and servitors to a strange and foreign prince'.[60] The departure of Irish Jacobite soldiers from Ireland to France after the Williamite War in 1691 was called the Flight of the Wild Geese. This most famous military diaspora in the history of Ireland occurred after the Battle of the Boyne following the agreement of the Treaty of Limerick. Because it was a common practice for Irish men to take part in foreign wars abroad between the 17th and 19th centuries, the term 'Wild Geese' generally referred to Irish soldiers who left for foreign armies. A substantial number of Irish soldiers existed in mainland American colonies, the British and non-British West Indies. Foreign armed forces particularly the European ones were often equipped with Irish regiments.

Irish men's bravery is well-documented across the globe. Irish regiments continuously played a crucial role throughout

European military history as they were often part of decisive battles. For example, many who fought in the Seven Years War in Holland became parliamentarians upon returning to Ireland. The Prince of Orange also remarked that Irish men were born soldiers. Apart from being a tradition, Irish people in general joined the army as they were attracted to the cause or out of necessity when they were in search of employment.

One of the earliest entries of Irish soldiers and the New World in the state papers is that in 1628, Sir Pierce Crosby made a proposal to the King for 'a grant of 5,000 l. out of the loan for Ireland, and two prize ships, to transport ten companies of the Irish regiment into a rich and fruitful part of America, not inhabited by any Christians; a good proportion of land to be grated to the undertaker'.

The British Army

From its inception, Irish people have always been an indispensable part of the British Army and Navy. For instance, a substantial number of Irish people went to mainland American colonies and served the British armed forces which greatly influenced the course of American history. When Captain John Cosnan of the 45th Foot recruited soldiers in Boston in 1758, the majority of Irish men were actually the people who had been fishing at Newfoundland. Irish men composed the largest single group of those men enlisted in New England. As they were highly mobile, many of them eventually came to the Caribbean to take part in various services. The Irish regiments of the British Navy and Army were always present in the Caribbean. All British West Indian regiments had Irish sergeants, corporals and drummers. According to the *Description and Succession Book of the Fourth West India Regiments,* 51 were Europeans and most of them were from Cork, Dublin, Tipperary, Galway and Waterford. They typically had more than one year of military service experience, while older sergeants had between 18 and 29 years of experience.

In order to call up a large number of soldiers, the recruitment of local indentured servants came naturally. But it was not unusual that some Irish Brigades in the Caribbean were in a rather dysfunctional state as the large majority of them recruited were not experienced soldiers but ordinary labourers. It is estimated that 3,300 freemen and indentured servants were enlisted and left Barbados for the Hispaniola-Jamaica expeditions of 1654-55. But only a few returned to Barbados because most of them died and the survivors decided to settle in Jamaica or elsewhere. As a result, between 1655 and 1683, the white population of Barbados fell from approximately 23,000 to 19,000, while Jamaica increased from 2,000 to more than 7,000 during the same period.

During the Battle of Havana in 1762, which was part of the Seven Years' War, Britain tried to take Spanish Havana. Typically, Irish officers and soldiers were fighting on both sides. Sir Boyle Roche from Galway was on the British side and hailed as a hero as he took part in the taking of Havana. He had a distinguished career with the British Army and became a politician in Ireland on his return. Britain ordered a Catholic Irish brigade of 6,000 men during the 1794-5 campaign in the Caribbean and 10 other Irish regiments were reserved for the expedition. Various Irish regiments from Cork and Dublin were present during the Windward and Leeward Islands campaigns. Irish servants' military drills constituted the island infantry and they wore red coats and black hats.

Like other officials, Governor Willoughby was gravely concerned that more than half of the 4,000 strong militia in Barbados were originally from Ireland. In 1667, he wrote to Charles II 'the keeping of slaves in subjection must still be provided for'. But gradually the military population decreased as they left the island. As a matter of fact, most of them couldn't stand the military drilling under the scorching sun. What's more, the mortality rate of soldiers was extremely high. A vast number of Irish soldiers died of malaria and yellow fever rather than from actual fighting. When the British invaded Saint Domingue (current Haiti) in 1793 in support of French slavers, they wanted to prevent a spill over to Jamaica. By 1798, they were forced out and more than half of the British troops that mainly consisted of Irish soldiers, who had embarked on this campaign, died of tropical diseases. After Emancipation in 1834, things started changing gradually. Indentured servants and artisans' jobs were all replaced by free Africans. But the militia's internal security functions such as quelling rebellions and an external defence force remained more or less the same, dominated by the white population.

In early days, the white population in Barbados consisted of a significant majority of soldiers but their numbers started decreasing along with the rising slave population. Like other islands, the militia was initially formed to protect the island from foreign invasions. But rather, in the case of Barbados, the problem came more from within as servant and/or slave rebellions occurred frequently. The way soldiers functioned was to manage rebellious servants and slaves until the official police force was established. After 1696, some 2,000 militia tenants were installed on Barbados plantations as a de facto police force.

Because there were too many militia tenants in Barbados, the militia bill passed in 1702 required plantations to send their parochial units one militia man for every 30 or 50 acres of land.[61] Each militia man without land could acquire a house and one or two acres of land on a leasehold basis for their services and to plant ground provisions and vegetables. They had to raise livestock and crops to sell in markets and often had contracts with the estates to provide the slaves with garments. Some of them also earned a living as waged workers namely as drivers, housekeepers, groomsmen, herdsmen, bookkeepers, managers, overseers, carpenters, plumbers, coopers, masons, ploughmen, coppersmiths, millwrights, wheelwrights and blacksmiths. The planters always held the positions of officers, while small holders, freemen and indentured servants made up the rank and file.

At the beginning, the military service was conducted all by white people in the British West Indian colonies. Local authorities knew that African people could be more efficient workers than the Irish but Irish soldiers were necessary for defence purposes. Therefore, all indentured servants had to serve in the militia under certain circumstances. According to a Barbados law of 1652, any one of them that could manfully fight like a true soldier should have half of his service remitted to him, and his master was to be reimbursed out of the public treasury. Jamaica increased the reward to complete freedom in 1673. Barbados started providing for the cure of wounded militiamen at public expense and for a grant of 2,000 pounds of sugar to them in 1685.

Since Jamaica was initially built and settled by soldiers, the Irish population in Jamaica consisted of mainly the poorer class soldiers and administrators at the beginning. The island was considered as a strategic location in the Caribbean and an established military system needed to be maintained. Major Robert Sedgwick who came to Jamaica in October 1655 to be in charge as Commissioner, observed: 'The soldiers left there had been principally drawn from the island of Barbados...we are forced to conclude that a really considerable number of Irish born, or at least of Irish descent must have found their way to Jamaica'.[62]

James Kelly was one of the Ulster Presbyterian agents who handled linen and Irish provisions in the ports. After spending 17 years in Jamaica working as a bookkeeper and tradesman, he published a book called *Voyage to Jamaica and Seventeen Years' Residence in That Island* in 1838 and wrote about the militia in Jamaica: 'Every free man, white, brown, & black, was required to be a soldier & every parish thus had its regiment of militia. On the sugar estates & coffee plantations, the white people were supplied with the necessary equipment a musket, &c. At the expense of the proprietors, with the exception of the red coat, – which the overseers, book-keepers, tradesmen, &c. Always had to purchase'.

William Stapleton from Tipperary is considered as one of the most significant military officers and governors. He served for the British King Charles II, assisted the re-conquering of Montserrat and ended up becoming governor of Montserrat, and eventually governed the whole British Leeward. He brought his friends and family members and supplied them with lands and official appointments. He himself married an heiress on Nevis which made his status solid.

Another significant administrator in Jamaica was called Thomas Lynch who arrived as part of Venables' army and became chief justice. He shortly became governor of Jamaica for the first time from 1663 to 1664, the second time from 1671 to 1674 and again for the last time from 1682 to 1684. When he arrived in Jamaica in 1681 to be governor for the third time, his wife Vere got seriously ill on the way. He had to leave her on her deathbed in Madeira. He also became very ill as soon as the ship entered the tropics and when he finally arrived in Jamaica, he had to be led to his first ceremonial engagements. He could hardly move for six days. He wrote: 'It is hardly possible to be alive and to have had more misfortunes than I have had this voyage'. By 1682, buccaneering had developed into piracy. He tried to suppress it by laws and repeated proclamations. The freebooters were offered an opportunity of returning to civilised pursuits. He struggled to introduce order and sobriety into the colony as the peace of the island were disturbed by 'La Trompeuse' and other French corsairs which sailed around Hispaniola. On top of this, Spanish corsairs continued to rob English vessels and refused to surrender English ships and goods, although he maintained a good relationship with the Spanish governors in the Caribbean by protecting Spanish merchant ships and receiving them in Jamaican ports. Nevertheless, continued Spanish hostility in the region against the English made it impossible to wipe out piracy in his life time. He died on 24 August 1684 in Jamaica.

Colonel Edward Doyley (or D'Oyley, Doyly, D'Oley) became governor of Jamaica between 1655 and 1662. He was not very interested in planting and trading but he was very efficient in maintaining order amongst men who were disheartened and averse to settlement. By the end of his service, he had developed the island as a thriving colony. One of his major achievements was his vigorous policy against the Spanish. He didn't only defend Jamaica but he encouraged privateers and carried the war into enemy territory. The military official William O'Brien, the Earl of Inchiquin was an Irish noble man who served as governor of Jamaica and Vice-Admiral of the Caribbean Seas from 1690 to 1692 until he died in Jamaica. He served various military forces in France and Spain under his father Murrough O'Brien. Those who served within the Caribbean include Major Smith Kelly, an Irish official who moved to Jamaica from St. Thomas in the 1680s.

The most captivating figure who almost changed the course of British and Irish history was British army officer and colonial administrator Edward Marcus Despard (1751-1803) from Laois. After joining the British army, he quickly attained the rank of colonel. After serving in Jamaica, he became governor of Roatan Island, off the Honduras coast. He also served on the British Mosquito Coast (Nicaragua/Honduras), Gulf of Honduras and Belize. He came back to London in the spring of 1790 at the beginning of the French Revolution. He joined various abolitionist movements to advocate the 'principles of freedom, of humanity, and of justice'.[63] He began to organise a conspiracy, a revolutionary army mutiny with a rising in London to assassinate King George III and capture the Tower of London and the Bank of England. Ultimately he planned to seize power in London and declare a republic. At the last minute, however, his plot was discovered and he and his revolutionaries which consisted of mostly Irish labourers, dockworkers, soldiers and sailors were arrested and executed. According to James Connolly, his conspiracy was tied to that of Robert Emmet, also of 1803; and like Emmet, he was an 'Irish apostle of a world-wide movement for liberty, equality and fraternity'.[64]

According to a newspaper article on 22 February 1803, when Colonel Despard was about to be hanged and beheaded, he was dressed in boots, a dark brown great coat with his hair unpowdered, as he ascended the gallows with great firmness. And he spoke in front of 20,000 people: 'Fellow Citizens, I come here, as you see, after having served my country, – faithfully, honourably, and usefully served it, for thirty years and upwards, to suffer death upon a scaffold for a crime of which I protest I am not guilty. I solemnly declare that I am no more guilty of it than any of you who may be now hearing me. – But, though his MAJESTY's Ministers know as well as I do, that I am not guilty, yet they avail themselves of a legal pretext to destroy a man, because he has been a friend to truth, to liberty, and to justice. Because he has been a friend to the poor and the oppressed. But, Citizens, I hope and trust, not withstanding my fate, and the fate of those who no doubt will soon follow me, that the principles of freedom, of humanity, and of justice, will finally triumph over falsehood, tyranny, and delusion, and every principle inimical to the interests of the human race'.[65]

Army surgeons

According to the list of the medical officers of the Army, Irish surnames were extensively listed. One of them include James Lynch O'Connor, an army surgeon for the Royal Artillery. After serving at the battle of Waterloo – the Anglo-Irish Duke of Wellington famously recruited countless Irish soldiers and won the battle in the end – he arrived in Port of Spain, Trinidad in 1817. He looked after Irish soldiers in the British Army on the island, such as the Connaught Rangers and the Inniskilling Fusiliers.

The Spanish Army

Joining foreign armed forces and operations was also a common way out for all Irish men as well as runaway servants. Irish soldiers were constantly serving the Spanish throughout the Americas. From 1585 onwards, they were serving at the Spanish garrison in Florida. There were quite a few high profile Irish officers in the Caribbean. Born in 1722, Baltrasna, County Meath, Alexander O'Reilly joined the Spanish Army as a cadet at the age of 11 and eventually climbed up to be lieutenant general. Often fighting against the British in the Caribbean, he is famous for building defences in Havana and Puerto Rico and managing to promote the fortunes of his fellow soldiers and countrymen there. When Britain negotiated favourable access to the Spanish colonies in the 1780s, a large number of Irish Catholics from Ireland, Britain and the British West Indies moved to the Spanish West Indies such as Puerto Rico.

The French Army

Irish soldiers were also indispensable in the French Army. Antoine Walsh's Irish brigade also served in the Caribbean. They were quite numerous in the French service when the Irish brigade of the French Army launched an expedition from Martinique to Saint Eustatia. When the French commander returned to Martinique, Colonel Thomas Fitzmaurice from Kerry was appointed Governor of Saint Eustatia. When the war ended, Fitzmaurice carried on serving in the French colonies such as Cayenne and Guadeloupe.

The Police Force

The militia functioned as an instrument to maintain order in the British West Indian colonies. Units of foot and horse existed chiefly to prevent inbred insurrection, especially in Barbados.

The British West Indian police force, notably the one in Barbados, largely consisted of Irish people who were former soldiers, indentured servants and poor whites in general. The first main Police Force in Barbados was officially established in 1835.

In Trinidad, the Royal Irish Constabulary was the model of the local policing system when it was established. In Jamaica, the local police force was modelled on the Irish one. The most prominent feature synonymous with the Irish was the red stripes or what Jamaicans normally referred to as a red seam on the trousers. The authorities tried to maintain British rule, all able-bodied freemen had to enlist in their local militia regiment. There were at least 8,000 enlisted men by 1802. Although it is not certain how many Irish people were included, it is believed a large number of them were originally from Ireland. The formal law enforcement in Jamaica began in 1716 when night watchmen were appointed to serve the cities namely Port Royal and Kingston, as well as the parishes of St. Catherine and St. Andrew. William Ramsay was appointed as inspector general when the first police force was established in 1832.

Sailors

Traditionally and historically, Irish sailors and marines served the Spanish fleet and the Royal Navy. Additionally, independent sailors were constantly recruited in Ireland during the height of the servant and slave trade. Most of the time, sailors initially got on a ship because they lived in the coastal region and had family members who were already working in the industry. Working as a sailor both on naval vessels and slave ships was rather a last resort because shipboard conditions were atrocious because of tough discipline, low wages, poor provisions and long confinement aboard ship. It was dangerous and disease-ridden, with extremely high mortality. They often got ill on board or died, and it was not uncommon to return home maimed. Nevertheless, life after at sea often meant just swapping to serve on pirate ships. That's why, a great many of pirates were Irish.

The reason why most of them initially became sailors, especially on slave ships, was they could not find any work elsewhere. Some people who struggled to earn a living namely ex-prisoners had no choice but to join the trade. After being recruited, the 'Articles of Agreement' contract needed to be signed by the men before joining the voyage. Quite often, sailors were teenagers, some only 13-years-old when they first got on a ship. Without education, they were often cheated of their wages and not able to write a will. If they died while on duty, their family members, wives and children back home in Ireland were often not properly paid and left destitute. Sailors were not only badly paid but were subject to brutal treatments and the voyage at sea was long and gruesome. Their working conditions were horrendous and often determined by ships' captains as they had absolute power over the ship and crew. Nasty captains of a slave ship commonly flogged and punished crew members as they pleased. One sailor's account reveals that because he took too much bread during a meal for the crew, he was whipped so hard and his clothes were torn to pieces by the captain. The captain always decided how much water and food were given to the sailors. According to the 1790 voyage of *Fame*, it was a pound and half of beef and half a pint of flour on Sundays. On Tuesday, two ounces of butter and four ounces of cheese were given. Each week, they had six pounds of bread and a quarter of a pint of spirits or half a pint of wine every day.

The mortality rate was more than 20% during a voyage. The slaves typically occupied below deck and sailors slept on the open deck for the whole voyage. Many died of tropical diseases such as malaria and yellow fever particularly on the West African coast, while African slaves got so-called European diseases such as measles and smallpox which spread quickly in their cramped conditions. Blindness of sailors were also common due to high fever or probably from looking directly into the sun to find the position of the ship at sea. In addition, they got often caught in sailors or slaves' uprisings.

Upon arriving in the Caribbean, merciless captains sometimes deserted sailors there who got weak due to the tropical heat or diseases, or even if they simply disliked them, without paying their wages or giving them their belongings. Although captains and ships' officers often punished slaves just for minor offences and raped female slaves on a regular basis, sailors were forbidden to treat the slaves poorly. Because of such inhumane working conditions, it had been highly difficult to recruit sailors by the 1780s. Without sailors, ships couldn't leave. Captains and pub landlords collaborated to deceive men into joining the voyage. For example, a gimmick worked like this: pub landlords would lend money to men for drinks to make them drunk. As they were too drunk and couldn't pay back the money, they had to work as sailors to repay the debt. They had to choose either to go to jail or get on a ship.

By the late 18th century, it is estimated at least 12 percent of sailors on slave ships from Liverpool were Irish. Irish sailors were travelling from both English ports and directly from Ireland to the Caribbean as Munster ports operated as the final stop for taking water and victuals before crossing the Atlantic since the 17th century.

The life on a Navy ship wasn't much better either. Eoghan Rua Ó Súilleabháin, also known as his anglicised name Owen Roe O'Sullivan (1748-1784), unwillingly served on an English naval vessel that reached Port Royal, Jamaica. Born in Kerry in 1748, he was a Gaelic language poet. By the time he was born, most of the native Irish in the southwest of Ireland had gone and emigrated. The Penal Laws were destroying the way local people lived and Catholic people were not given any rights nor opportunities. The Navy life did not suit him at all. He was on a ship and sailed under Admiral George Rodney for the British West Indies as 'one of those thousands of barbarously mistreated seamen'. He famously wrote an English-language ballad called

'Rodney's Glory' celebrating a British naval victory in the Caribbean. He was desperate to quit and wrote his one and only poem in English to persuade his Royal Navy commander to allow him to leave the service.

Pirates

There are several ways to describe those who were operating and making a living on the sea: pirates, privateers and buccaneers. By definition, pirates sailed in ships, attacked ships and ports, then stole from them. It was illegal. Privateers were any individual people who were granted license by authorities and governments to attack enemy ships. Basically the way pirates and privateers functioned was the same but the legal term was different. Privateers were officials. A buccaneer was a general term for a pirate or privateer operating in the Caribbean during the late 17th and the early 18th centuries. The term buccaneer was derived from *viande boucanée* in French which means smoked meat, the process of curing strips of meat by smoking over a slow fire. Spain was the first comer in the Caribbean and eventually other European nations such as France, England and the Netherlands started fighting for territories and power in the region. Local people, native inhabitants and vagrants who caught wild animals, preserved and cooked the meat to sell to passing ships around Hispaniola, or offered European ships and settlements water and smoked meat. However, they eventually turned to piracy and terrorised the Caribbean. Buccaneers, the meat sellers, developed into full-blown pirates in the Caribbean. They were usually a lawless group of people consisted of shipwrecked sailors, marooned sailors and runaway indentured servants. It was often a way of earning a living.

Quite a few notorious Irish pirates existed in the Caribbean, particularly during the period of the land confiscations of Irish Catholics when so-called 'banished people' were forced to be at sea. Other people joined in piracy after leaving from English ships, being recruited by local people at Irish ports. Historically, there had been always an active pirate community in Ireland such as in Youghal and Kinsale which served as a link to mainland America and the Caribbean.

Some of the major piracy strongholds in the Caribbean during the 17th century were Port Royal, Jamaica; the Bahamas; Tortuga; Providence Island. The Bahamas islands were not suitable for agriculture with the arid climate and thin soil but strategically located. New Providence shortly became a vital base of operations for British and Irish pirates. After the earthquake of 1692 which destroyed Port Royal, the surviving pirates based in Jamaica and Tortuga (Haiti) moved to the Bahamas. Local people in the Bahamas supported their activities and proprietary governors of Carolina who were granted the Bahamas by Charles II also assisted them. The authorities sold them commissions as privateers with the right to attack enemy ships. As a result, there were thousands of former privateers who lost their livelihood due to the Treaty of Utrecht that ended the War of the Spanish Succession but soon started their old trade again. At one point, piracy around the Leeward Islands were uncontrollable. They didn't just attack ships in the ocean but also on land. By 1713, there had been more new pirates operating at sea.

Many privateers, namely the ones siding with the French, fought against England. In 1678, approximately 800 pirates landed at St Christopher and fought to support the French. There was an English frigate with 300 soldiers on board in 1683 which carried three full years' provisions. London ordered the frigate to fight piracy. An Antiguan planter reported on the situation in the Leeward Islands in 1695: 'This part of the world is full of privateers. The French have fourteen small craft with six hundred men in them, which are daily watching these islands, and know all that passes as well as ourselves'.[66] As always, Irish people at sea could be found on both sides. One of the most famous buccaneers in the Caribbean was John Murphy, aka Don

Juan Morf. He was the master sergeant in Tortuga but fled to Cartagena, a city on the Caribbean coast side in Colombia. He is believed to be the same person as Don Juan de Morfa Geraldino who was admiral of the fleet which attacked Tortuga in 1654.

Roman Catholic Philip Fitzgerald was both a privateer and pirate. He served the Spanish in the Caribbean and obtained a commission as a privateer out of Havana in 1672. He successfully captured several English vessels and killed the people on board. He was notorious because of the atrocious way he treated and killed English sailors. Regarding his barbaric abuse to English captives, he once remarked: 'Giving no reason but that his countrymen were ill-used by the English 24 years ago, and he should never be satisfied with English blood, but could drink it as freely as water'. Eventually, England ordered he be hunted down in 1675 and his head delivered from Havana. But no record of him being captured by the English exists. A man called 'Red Legs' Greaves, was a former indentured servant in Barbados and a former soldier in the Catholic Confederation Army. As he was refused amnesty to go to Spain with the others. He managed to escape his horrendous indentured life and became a pirate. He eventually retired from piracy and settled in Nevis as a planter. Darby Mullins from Derry was sold to a planter in the British West Indies at 18 because he was an orphan. He also managed to escape his indentured life in Barbados, and joined Captain Kidd's (Scottish) piracy but he was eventually captured and hanged in New York in 1701. An Irish pirate called Plunkett stole a ship off Barbados and entered Bridgetown harbour, and destroyed some of the fortifications in 1650. He is probably the man Plunquet who is described in Ligon's book *A True and Exact History of the Island of Barbados*: 'On 15 April 1650 at midnight: which time our master made choyce of that he might better pass undescryed by a well known pirate, that had for many days layn hovering about the island, to take any ships that traded with London, by virtue of a commission as he pretended, from the Marquis of

Ormond. This pirate was an Irish man, his name Plunquet, a man bold enough; but had the Character of being more merciless and cruel then became a valiant man'.

George Cusack was an infamous pirate in Europe and the Caribbean in the late 17th century.

After his failed attempts at mutiny, he was captured and spent some time in Marshalsea prison in Southwark, London where debtors, pirates and smugglers were incarcerated. He was a sailor and gunner on various ships, and served as a privateer for England during the Anglo-Dutch Wars. He seized various prizes and had been doing great as a successful pirate. But after the wars ended, he seized an English ship and tried to sell it while he left its crew on the previously captured ship adrift. He was eventually captured by the English and came back to Marshalsea prison where he was hanged in 1675. Richard Noland (or Holland, or Nowland) was an Irish-born pirate who famously sailed with Samuel Bellamy, an English pirate. He was hired by Captain Benjamin Hornigold during the War of Spanish Succession and eventually worked as Hornigold's agent at Nassau, recruiting men and looking after his financial interests during Hornigold's absence. He soon took up service with the Spanish. Noland successfully served as a privateer for Spain in the Caribbean. While sailing to the Mediterranean for the Battle of Cape Passaro, several Spanish vessels were captured. Noland was able to escape with fellow Irishman Admiral George Cammock and returned to the Caribbean to work as a privateer for Spain again. Dennis McCarthy who was born in Ireland was a prize fighter and pirate. He was captured and hanged at the age of 28 in New Providence, the Bahamas, in 1718.

The most popular female pirate of all time in the Caribbean was Anne Bonny. She was born in Cork in 1700 and her birth name was Anne McCormac. She was an illegitimate child, the daughter of Mary Brennan, a servant and her employer, lawyer William McCormac. She had red hair and was raised as a boy.

Her father called her Andy. He eventually took his child and her mother to South Carolina and established himself in Charleston as a planter and merchant. He allegedly dropped the original 'Mc' prefix of the family name to blend into America. Anne made a name for herself in the colonies by beating a would-be rapist within an inch of his life and then by running off to join the pirates. Then, she married a poor sailor and pirate called James Bonny who probably hoped to acquire her father's possession but Anne had already been disowned by her father by that time. Sometime between 1714 and 1718, Anne and James moved to Nassau on New Providence Island in the Bahamas which was known as a sanctuary for English pirates, also called the Republic of Pirates. It was here she met John 'Calico Jack' Rackham, captain of the pirate sloop *Revenge*. They became lovers and had a son in Cuba. She divorced her husband, married Rackham, and they started the pirate life together. Bonny, Rackham and Mary Read, a fellow female English pirate, aka Mark Read, stayed in Jamaica and the surrounding seas for a while, capturing quite a few vessels. In October 1720, their luck ran out as Rackham and his crew were attacked by a 'King's ship', a sloop ordered by Nicholas Lawes, Governor of Jamaica. Lawes successfully hunted down and tried a score of pirates during the Golden Age of Piracy. Rackham was hanged, Bonny and Read 'pleaded their bellies' receiving a temporary stay of execution until they gave birth. Read died in prison but no historical record of Bonny's release or of her hanging exist. Because of her father's influence, it is widely believed that she was released and returned to Carolina.

Port Royal

Located at the mouth of the Kingston Harbour in Jamaica, Port Royal was an industrious city with artisans and merchants but most famously, as the home of pirates. It was initially founded in 1518 by the Spanish and developed into the largest port city in the Caribbean. It functioned as the centre of shipping and commerce and as a hub base for pirates. Strategically located to seize Spanish wealth, thousands of privateers and pirates found Port Royal appealing because of its proximity to trade routes, especially the Spanish Main, or surrounding regions within the Caribbean Sea and the Gulf of Mexico within Spain's New World Empire. As the location allowed them easy access to prey, it was used as an ideal base for launching raids on Spanish settlements.

As Spain repeatedly tried to recapture Jamaica, Governor Doyley asked the Brethren of the Coast to make Port Royal their home port in 1657. The Brethren was a coalition of buccaneers that concentrated on attacking Spanish ships. They were legitimately hired by the government to function as English privateers. England successfully established a system of defence in Port Royal. One of the most famous privateers was Henry Morgan. Originally from Wales, he came to Barbados as an indentured servant in the 1640s. When his indenture was completed, he became a buccaneer because he couldn't receive land nor find a decent job on the island. In 1674, England gave him a title and he became Colonel Morgan, lieutenant governor of Jamaica, senior member of Council and commander-in-chief of the military forces. He famously attacked Panama from Port Royal, and looted the coastal settlements of Cuba, Hispaniola (Dominican Republic) and Central America. The harbour was large enough to accommodate various types of vessels. The authorities in Port Royal often complained to the King of their losses from pirates. But at the same time, the English didn't have sufficient troops to protect themselves from external attack, so Jamaican governors used pirates to defend the city.

By the 1660s, Port Royal had effectively become the most lawless English colony. With its residents mainly consisting of pirates, prostitutes and cutthroats and it had earned a reputation as the 'Sodom of the New World'. To cater to its residents' needs, a wide range of entertainments were available. There were many places to lodge; taverns, brothels, and coffee houses. The port kept bulls and bears for sport at the bear garden, as well as having assorted fun activities such as billiards, cockfighting and shooting at the target. The English diarist John Taylor described it as 'the most wicked and sinful city in the world'. Another observer wrote of the island 'the Dunghill of the Universe populated exclusively by prostitutes, convicts and drunks'.

As early as 1671, governor Thomas Lynch observed that so much land in the town had been granted that it was 'rendered unhealthy, for want of streets and public commodities'. It is estimated there were nearly 8,000 inhabitants who were Irish, English, Scottish, Jewish, French, Miskito Indians, Spanish and Africans. They were merchants, tavern owners, churchmen, a regiment of 2,500 men and 4,000 slaves and 'women of ill-repute'. Particularly, taverns, cock fighting pits and brothels flourished. The financial stimulus was provided by the buccaneers on a regular basis. They enjoyed themselves and when they ran out of money, they went to sea, until it lasted. In June 1692, an horrendous earthquake destroyed much of sin city sliding into the sea. Two-thirds of the city sank and more than 2,000 were killed. As a refuge for survivors, Kingston was founded.

Chapter 3

Caribbean islands

By 1630, Irish people had already been living in the Caribbean who mostly arrived in their own right. A massive influx of the Irish in the region meant they were at one point the majority in some islands. They named their settlements after the cities they came from and quite a few Irish Towns existed. For instance, just to name a few, there is an Irish Town in St Andrew, Kildare and Clonmel in St. Mary and Belfast and Middleton in St. Thomas in Jamaica; there is an Irish Town in St Christopher; Cork Hill, Fogharty Hill, Kinsale and Harris Lookout in Montserrat. Each island in the British West Indies shared common history to a certain degree but they all developed their own socio-economics, plantation society and political cultures.

Topography

Montserrat, St Christopher and Nevis have a mountainous topography with rugged terrains and they are also volcanic, while Barbados is relatively flat. The biggest British possession, Jamaica has mountains, rivers and diverse ecosystems. The size of each island is: Barbados 166 square miles; Montserrat: 40 square miles; Nevis: 36 square miles; Jamaica: 4,400 square miles. All the colonies in the British West Indies constantly suffer from natural disasters such as hurricanes and earthquakes. For example, some major earthquakes toppled Jamestown, Nevis into the sea in 1680, and the former vibrant capital city Port Royal, Jamaica sank below sea level in 1692.

St Christopher

In 1493, Christopher Columbus arrived and claimed the island for Spain. A French Huguenot settlement was established at

Dieppe Bay in 1538 but shortly they were kicked out by the Spaniards. St Christopher was the first English possession in the Caribbean. The island was claimed by the Spanish but unoccupied, so the English took it and established its colony in 1623 and the French also took a part in 1625. The island had been split into English and French jurisdictions from the beginning. The French relinquished the island and it became affiliated with the Kingdom of Great Britain in 1783.

An explorer from Suffolk Sir Thomas Warner was the founder and governor of St Christopher. He knew that farming tobacco was highly profitable after spending some time learning how it could grow in the Amazon. With its perfect strategic location, he thought St Christopher could be profitable for agriculture as it had fertile soil, abundant fresh water and safe anchorage. Initially, he brought some English and Irish migrant workers from the Amazon. Charles I issued a royal commission confirming Warner authority over St Christopher and also later the islands of Nevis, Montserrat and Barbados. A merchant Ralph Merrifield provided the capital, and settlers were recruited to develop the colony.

From its inception, the British occupied the centre of the island and the French took up the eastern and western ends but the borders were rather porous. The Irish were forbidden to practice Catholicism within the English territory but the French side was served by the Capuchin order. When Father Stritch, an Irish Jesuit from Limerick arrived in 1650, he intentionally built a chapel in Capesterre in the French colony Saint-Christophe, very close to the border with the English St Christopher side so that Irish Catholics could cross the border easily. Father Stritch shortly moved to Montserrat to offer Mass in the forest disguised as a woodcutter. By cutting down a few trees every day, the area looked as if a lumbering camp was in operation. He travelled between St Christopher and Montserrat at intervals until he moved back to Ireland in 1660 when another Irish priest John

Grace replaced him. Just like Father Stritch, Father John Grace of the diocese of Cashel served in St Christopher and Montserrat sporadically.

One of the earliest Irish settlers who arrived with the English was Gregory French of Galway. About 150 passengers were picked up from Kinsale in 1634 who arrived in St Christopher. Passage was typically six pounds per person, and the freight of goods from Ireland to St Christopher, or elsewhere in the Caribbean was three to four pounds per ton.

England tried to recruit more labourers as it needed to develop the newly acquired colony. In order to escape poverty and political disturbance in Ireland, St Christopher quickly became a very popular destination for Irish Catholics to emigrate to. According to the High Court of Admiralty papers, Captain Thomas Anthony was supposed to fill up 120 Irish passengers in Kinsale for Virginia in 1636. But Irish labourers refused to go there as they were well informed about better wages in the British West Indies. As a result, he had to change his shipping plans and made St Christopher his final destination. According to various witnesses' accounts, Dutch ships often recruited and transported a large number of Irish people from Kinsale to St Christopher.

One of the pioneer settlers was Captain Peter Sweetman who left Ireland to be a planter on St Christopher in 1641. As a subject of the British King Charles I, he had contacts with various merchants who used ports in Cork and Kinsale. Sweetman brought many farmers, women and soldiers to 'settle and open up the land' on the English side of St Christopher. Around this time, the Bishop of Tuam, Malachy O'Queely, also noted the departure of 600 emigrants with two priests from Galway.

After England acquired other Leeward Islands such as Nevis, Antigua and Montserrat, the Irish from St Christopher were encouraged to settle across the new British West Indian colonies. By 1639, approximately 3,000 Irish Catholics had been living in the Leeward Islands. Political events at home always had a severe impact on the British West Indies. News of the 1641 rebellion in Ireland which began as an attempted coup d'etat by the Irish Catholic gentry against the Protestants, spread across the British West Indian colonies. On St Christopher, fights broke out between the Irish and the English and its governor tried to get rid of the Irish by shipping them to Montserrat. Quite a few Irish people escaped rising anti-Catholic feeling by fleeing into French or Spanish territories.

There had been about 25,000 Irish on St Christopher and Nevis by 1650. On 6 June, 1666, a group of Irish people tried to take St Christopher but the attempt failed. According to the state paper: 'Lieut-Col. Morgan and the rest of the Leeward forces against a well fortified house, where 200 men well armed received them with much resolution and wounded and killed most of the buccaneers and the Irish in the rear (always a bloody and perfidious people to the English Protestant interest) fired volleys into the front and killed more than the enemy of our own forces'. Later in 1666, Irish servants and freemen on St Christopher celebrated the declaration of war between England and France by rising up against the English planters. It was the Irish who helped the French to take control of the island by evicting 800 English planters.

When the island shifted to sugar, it needed more labourers to work at labour intensive sugar plantations. The sugar planters typically preferred African slaves as they were more cost-effective and productive than problematic Irish indentured servants. The large-scale systematic slave trade had begun and ships arrived via Barbados. The voyage from Barbados to St Christopher took about three days. It was difficult to travel at night because if a ship veered too close to other islands on the Atlantic side, they could smash into outcroppings of rock or sudden squalls could whip down the steep mountain sides and overturn them.

African manual labourers pushed the Irish servants up the

social hierarchy.

Overall, early indentured servants all did very well. An English planter Christopher Jeaffreson in St Christopher wrote a letter to his cousin in England in 1677: 'Slaves live as well now as the servants did formerly. The white servants are so respected that, if they will not be too refractory, they may live much better than thousands of the poor people in England, during their very servitude, or at least as well'.[67] The amount of a servant's bounty was fixed at 10 pounds in those days: 'I confess all servants are very acceptable here; and if any laborious and industrious men would transport themselves, I should gladly receive them and allow them the customs of the country, with meate, drinke, lodging and clothing, as are necessarie; but it is not the custome to promesse any more than three hundred pounds of sugar at the end of their term of four years'.[68]

The capital of the island, Basseterre, quickly became a popular entertainment destination for European visitors from neighbouring islands, especially Montserrat. St Christopher offered dinner parties, dancing, cards, picnics, cockfighting and amateur performances such as King Lear and Othello and dancing masters and music teachers were available to teach the children.[69] There was once a settlement of Irish people in the capital Basseterre and the area called Irish Town still exists. The Irish labourer class had disappeared by 1700 as they moved up to the class of artisans and overseers or emigrated. Britain won the War of the Spanish Succession (1701-1714) and the French eventually left from Saint-Christophe. The island was renamed Saint Kitts but it was not able to develop as fast as it could mainly due to continuous political instability.

Barbados

Barbados has a special place in Irish people's heart, according to an Irish diplomat who was interviewed in a documentary called *The Redlegs: Ireland's Sugar Slaves of Barbados*. Produced by TG4, the Gaelic-language television station in 2009. Dr. Edmond Molloy, Consul General of Barbados explained: 'It's an interesting thing, even today, if you ask somebody, what would you do if you win a lottery, the first thing to come out is Barbados. So Barbados is somewhere in the folk memory here in Ireland'. According to him, Barbados had been their dream destination, not Jamaica or Montserrat.

The indigenous people of Barbados were Amerindians who arrived from Venezuela and made home along the coast. Under the command of Captain John Power, an English ship came to the island on 14 May 1625. In the name of King James I, Barbados was claimed and it was officially colonised in 1627. This was the second English colony in the Caribbean. A wealthy London merchant, William Courteen (1572–1636) financed the colonisation of Barbados.

What makes this island unique is its geographical location. It is somewhat isolated from the other islands and quite self-contained. Because of the location, east of the main Antillean chain, the island was used as the first Caribbean port of call for all ships from Europe and Africa. Without being attacked by the Caribs, the Spanish and the French, Barbados was able to develop itself as the richest and most populous of the British West Indies during the 17th century.

In fact, British people valued this island so much and often called it a 'fair jewel'. English people genuinely thought the scenery reminded them of England. The dense tropical forest that originally covered the island was all cleared during the first four decades of settlement to establish plantations. With no mountains or rivers, the island was relatively flat. Sir. Henry Colt, a member of the Essex gentry, visited Barbados in 1631 and wrote that it reminded him of the gently rolling hills and green fields of England. The early planters often found Barbados more hospitable than the other islands. That's why Barbados was affectionately called 'Little England' or 'English island' in the

17th century.

Its coral limestone soil is thin but fertile and its annual rainfall averages more than sixty inches. Corn, cassava, plantains and yams were abundant. There were lots of wild pigs and animals. Barbados was often acclaimed the 'richest spote of ground in the worlde', 'the sweet spot of earth' and 'the key of the West Indies'. Despite all the political, economic and social hardships, there was plenty of food, and the population grew rapidly in the 1630s. Barbados evolved into 'the most flourishing colony the English have in the world'. Shortly, the wealthy planters lived in extravagant mansions and 'spread every day with variety of nice dishes, enjoyed magnificent chairs, chaises, and all the conveniences for their travelling, and spent conspicuously on their dress which was fashionable and courtly'.[70]

Barbados was considered as an indispensable military base as the prevailing trade winds allowed ships from Barbados to reach other parts of the Caribbean and the Americas quickly, although reaching Barbados from the west took more time. As the first British West Indian island to successfully shift to sugar, Barbados shortly became economically powerful.

Irish indentured servants

By the middle decades of the 17th century, Barbados already had a higher population density than anywhere in the British Empire excluding London. In 1634, Andrew White, an English Jesuit visited Barbados and observed that some Catholics were both English and Irish.

In 1635, many of the 985 settlers who arrived in Barbados from London were indentured servants. 91 percent of them were single people in their teens and early twenties hoping to receive between two and 10 acres apiece when their indentures expired.

In 1636, ships at Kinsale were recruiting servants for St Christopher. But the captain of one of the ships – there were more women than men – decided to go to Barbados as the island needed more workers. It was common for captains to change destinations. In the end, 56 Irish people from Kinsale arrived. After the Cromwellian conquest of Ireland, the island was suddenly swarmed with a large influx of indentured servants. In 1652, the majority of 12,000 so called political prisoners on Barbados were Irish. An Englishman Henry Whistler came to the island in 1655 and witnessed the white population on the island consisted of Irish, English, Scottish, French, Spanish and Dutch. Barbados at one point had a substantial number of Irish people, more than Montserrat or Jamaica, but Barbados didn't become the most Irish colony in the British West Indies because by the time many early servants had served their indentures, they obtained land and status, and became pretty much absorbed into the British population. Additionally, the majority of them left for other Caribbean islands both British and non-British, mainland America, Suriname or elsewhere in search of land and freedom.

Population

While estimates vary, the population could be up to 30,000 white residents, most of them militia and indentured servants on Barbados in the late 1640s. It is estimated more than half of the 4,000-strong Barbadian militia consisted of Irishmen. There is no official record but some historians estimate more than 50 percent of residents in Barbados in the 17th century at one point were probably Irish. After Irish servants caused rebellions, the Barbados Assembly refused to allow merchants to bring Irish people during Daniel Searle's administration from 1652 to 1660. But Oliver Cromwell didn't stop transporting them en masse. According to some estimates, by 1684, there had been 19,568 white residents, 2,381 white servants, 5,911 militiamen and African slaves were 46,602. The growth of a slave-based economy gradually shrank economic opportunities for freed former Irish servants in the British West Indies. The white population started decreasing rapidly around 1680 as the land on Barbados was all taken up and there was no incentive or prospects to make them stay. As a result, Barbados's white population shrank from 30,000 in the early 1650s to less than 17,000 in 1715, while the population of enslaved Africans had increased from about 20,000 in 1655 to nearly 42,000 by 1712. By 1740, indentured servants were no longer the most significant group as the number of them fell below a few hundred. Former indentured servants who started their Caribbean life as humble labourers moved up the social ladder by joining slave controlling professions such as militia tenants, overseers, slave catchers, officers in the militia and administrators in the Council. In most cases, they had become slave-holding planters within their life time.

Wills

It was a common practice for planters to leave a will and many of them are recorded. The great number of former Irish indentured servants eventually became land and slave owners, and left money and possessions upon their deaths. On Barbados, for instance, the Irish planters who left wills include Dermon Mollony, Patrick Browne, Dermon Conniers, Dennis Murfee, Daniell Maccolin, Cornelius Bryan, Dinis Sullivan, Teague Murfee, Teige Connell and the list is endless. According to the 1680 census, Teague Murfee had five acres of land and five 'negroes' in his household. His will states that he was married to Katherine, had one daughter, Margarett, and had a granddaughter fathered by his recently deceased son, James. The names of the enslaved people he owned are: Franke, Judy, Loggen, Sheela and Maria. In his 1688 will, Teige Connell, probably a wage earner or small-scale farmer, left between three and 10 pounds sterling to four people, and another pound and muscovado sugar to his family and friends. He also mentioned that his cousin Daniel was serving his time as an indentured servant.

In many cases, planters bequeathed their possessions to his Irish servants. The Davis Collection of Barbadian documents include a planter's will, dated 1 May 1657: 'I give to my Christian servants, Desmond O'Doyle and Hannah, six months a piece of their times, provided that they doe continue Dutyfull servants to my wife; but if they be anyways disobedient or refractory, then this bequest to be voyde and of none effect. And, unto Desmond O'Doyle, I give my best suite of clothes and my best hatt'. Although, this is apparently an exception to the general rule of 'severity that existed in the treatment of white labour in Barbados which was generally a disgrace to the English name'.[71]

The Successful Irish

One of the most remarkable examples is Cornelius Bryan who bounced back and became comfortable in his lifetime. A musician, a piper by profession arrived in Barbados in the 1650s. He was a waged labourer, not a bond labourer. He was accused of slandering English officials by threatening to drink their blood: 'If there was so much English blood in the tray as there was meat, I would eat it'.[72] Because of this comment he made, he was sentenced under a statute recommending corporal punishment 'on such persons as give out mutinous language'. He received 21 lashes on his bare back at the Indian Bridge – constructed by the Indians and later the capital city Bridgetown was named after this bridge – by the common hangman before the prison in Bridgetown. Despite the punishment, he carried on with mutinous language and he was eventually sentenced to deportation. He was ordered to leave Barbados within the month. In 1678, there was a Cornelius Bryan living on the 'Irish island' and another at Palmetto Point on nearby St Christopher.[73] Cornelius Bryan is not an uncommon name, but it is possible he probably never has been deported at all. There was a Cornelius Bryan, a member of the planter or merchant class, who made a will in Barbados in 1687. Nearly 30 years later, when he died in Barbados, he owned slaves and property like a typical English planter. According to the 1680s census, he acquired two servants and nine slaves to work for his small estate in St. James Parish. His will states that he bequeathed everything to his wife Margaret and six children, Alice, Cornelius, Katherine, James, Jeremiah and Daniel, 22 acres of land, a feather bed, a cedar chest, a black horse, and 13 African slaves Betty, Grace, Tomy, Mingo, George, Anah, Old Pegg, Venus, Pegg, Nell, Jack, Young Tomy and Cain.

To the majority of people, Barbados, the first stop, was a stepping stone. Samuel Watt, a Presbyterian from Donegal, went to Barbados in his twenties in 1801 and then moved to Kingston, Jamaica. In 1808, he had a partnership with Mr. Cummings who wanted to start a business relationship which would allow him to make a trip to Ireland. He did not amass massive wealth but did relatively well throughout the Caribbean. When was in his forties, his health started declining and he finally decided to return to Ireland in 1825. He died there in 1826.

Nevis

Separated by a two-mile channel called 'the narrows', St Christopher and a smaller island Nevis were valuable islands for the English in the 17th century. With one great mountain, Nevis had less farmland than St Christopher. Amongst the Leeward Islands, Nevis was the first to convert from tobacco to sugar. Although the Spanish claimed Nevis, actual European settlement did not happen until Anthony Hilton moved there from St Christopher for the first time in around 1625. The English merchant Hilton obtained financial backing from some wealthy Irish merchants, and arrived in Nevis accompanied by 80 Irish settlers from St Christopher and Nevis was officially declared as an English colony in 1628. Hilton became the first Governor of Nevis.

When Spain invaded Nevis in 1629, Irish indentured servants on the island encouraged the Spanish attackers. Nevis became the headquarters for the Royal African Company in 1675 and functioned as the slave market within the Leeward Islands. It is estimated between 6,000 and 7,000 Africans came through en route to other islands every year.

According to a census of 1678, Irish people consisted of 22% of the population, most of them were indentured servants and freemen. Nevis was the seat of the Leeward Islands colony and remained the colonial capital for the Leeward Islands until 1698 when the seat was transferred to Antigua for military reasons. In 1700, 20 percent of the British Empire's total sugar production was from plantations in Nevis. During this period, Nevis was the most productive British Leeward Island. Just like other British West Indies, white indentured servants started decreasing due to increased wages in England and less incentive to migrate to or stay in the British West Indian colonies. By 1780s, 90 percent of nearly 10,000 people on Nevis had been Africans.

Montserrat

The first European who arrived in Montserrat was Christopher Columbus in 1493. He named the island after the monastery of *Santa Maria de Monserrate* in the Catalan mountains. The early settlers in Montserrat included some Irish people who were brought from the Amazon probably around 1631. The island came under English control in 1632 when anti-Catholic violence in Nevis broke out. In 1633, disaffected Irish Catholics from St Christopher and indentured servants from Ireland arrived. Other early Irish Catholics settlers included the Irish who had been kicked out of Virginia. According to a report by an English Jesuit Andrew White: 'The inhabitants of Montserrat are Irishmen who were expelled by the English of Virginia for the profession of the Catholic faith'.[74]

Almost Ireland

Father White who came to the Leeward Island in the mid-1630s observed that there were already a visible number of Irish Catholic people living in Montserrat. In 1634, Montserrat was described by Father White as 'a noble plantation of Irish Catholics'. According to some estimate, 70 percent of whites on Montserrat were Irish in 1637. Anthony Briskett (or Brisket, Bryskett), a Protestant Irish who became the first governor of Montserrat and the main coloniser of this island brought some settlers from Ireland. By 1650, commercial ties between Ireland and Montserrat had been solidly established. Tobacco, sugar and indigo were shipped to Ireland on a regular basis. In 1665, the Irish population was at its height and in 1666, there were six Irish to every colonist in Montserrat. Because there were simply too many Irish people, an English governor in 1668 described it as 'almost an Irish colony'. In 1678, the Irish were still numerous as they made up 69 percent of the white population of Montserrat. They were overwhelmingly Catholic, indentured servants and waged freemen. According to the census in 1678, the white population of the island was 2,682, of whom 1,644 were indentured servants. The majority of planters and government officials were both Irish Protestants and Catholics. The island turned into a microcosm of Ireland – with its English overlords and Protestant Irish, or New English families at the top of the hierarchy, the dispossessed gentry of Munster and Connacht formed a planter and trader elite, then the smallholders and indentured servants. In the Caribbean, however, there was another layer below, the African slaves.

Irish governors

Under the governorship of the Leeward Islands and Barbados (until 1671), each island had a form of representative government. Administrator William Stapleton served as governor of the Leeward Islands, and deputy governor of Montserrat. Stapleton initially arrived as his family estates in Ireland were confiscated by Cromwellian soldiers. After settling in Montserrat, he made all sorts of practical improvements to build the newly planted colony. He reformed the system of land tenure, regulated its currency and increased its trade and erected an Anglican church to replace that of Anthony Briskette (or Brisket, Briskett) an Irish Protestant from Wexford. Briskette was the first governor of Montserrat who owned property and had business associates in Virginia. According to Catholic historian Aubrey Gwynn, Briskette also recruited many Irish people from Munster, such as Collins, Barry, Sullivan, Roche, Cormack, Callaghan, Driscoll and Ryan to settle in Montserrat.

Freedom of religion

Penal laws existed within the British system which prevented Catholics from holding office and public practice of their religion was banned. In 1756, the first resident Dominican priest Father Lynch arrived in Montserrat and mass was being celebrated in private houses of wealthy Catholics, such as the Hamilton family. At the beginning, building a church was outlawed but the first Catholic church was built in 1852.[75] Unlike Ireland under the penal laws, Catholicism was not the biggest obstacle in Montserrat as Catholics had more freedom. Compared to other British West Indian islands, Montserrat somewhat allowed freedom of religion as they were able to purchase land and hold certain professions. In most cases, Irish Catholics benefited from the growing Atlantic trade. Former indentured Irish Catholics eventually obtained land, slaves, plantations and were freely involved with all kinds of mercantile activities.

Climbing up the ladder

The New World generally offered various opportunities for all. Overall, the large majority of indentured servants from Ireland became relatively well-off within their lifetime in the British West Indies and did particularly well in Montserrat. In many cases, Irish indentured servants became smallholders and lived mainly by renting out their slaves. For example, Garret Fahy owned 16 slaves, four horses and one cultivated acre. Anthony

Bodkin had no land but 13 slaves. Labourer John Conner had two slaves, a man and a woman. Contrary to popular belief, the majority of Irish people came to Montserrat of their own will with capital and ambition.

Privileged people like David Galway (or Gallway, Galloway, Gallaway) acquired wealth and positions almost instantly. He came from Cork in the 1660 with resources and became a major in the island militia. He acquired a substantial amount of wealth, the island's most extensive estate, 1,400 acres in St. Patrick's parish, on the south west slopes of the Soufriere Hills, stretching from the sea to the top of the mountains. It was part sugar plantation and part cattle ranch. By the late 1670s, he was serving on the Montserrat Council, an appointed position normally given only to prominent landowners. By 1729, the family estate had been one of the largest on the island. The majority of the 311 Irish who lived in 59 households on or close to his land in 1673 lived on the barren, windswept slopes to the south of the sugar works on small plots where they kept goats, sheep and pigs. Initially impoverished Irish residents, waged labourers, subsistence farmers and small artisans who owned little or no land and no houses lived in the rocky lands of St. Patrick's Parish in the south. They were Mulrains, Ryans, Sweenys and Barrys. According to the 1677 census, more than 40 percent of the total island population lived there. They were almost all Irish people who lived on less than 10 percent of the total island territory, on poor and dry land. Galway's sugar plantation was doing well for a while but it started declining between the 1670s and 1720s. According to the 1729 census, the Galway family had no white servants and only 62 slaves. As the African population started taking over, the majority of Irish people emigrated.

Sugar creates wealth

Compared with other British West Indian islands, Montserrat was slow to shift to sugar from tobacco, indigo and provision.

By 1680, sugar finally had taken off and dominated the island. Because sugar came late, African slaves also came late. According to some statistics, there were 523 African slaves in 1671. In 1678, there were 1,894 Africans and 1,845 Irish. During the first decade of the 18th century, there were 3,570 Africans in Montserrat; 6,063 Africans and 641 Irish in 1729; and 9,834 Africans in 1775. As more Africans arrived, Irish people rose and became economically more powerful. Montserrat eventually developed quality sugar in the British West Indies. Consequently, the majority of Irish households owned slaves by 1678 and almost all Irish people had slaves by 1729.

In 1701, conflicts broke out in the Leeward Islands amongst European colonists. Planters in Montserrat lost about 180,000 pounds and many residents were left destitute by the invasion. Wealthy Irish planters also suffered losses. For instance, Bartholomew Lynch 2,675 pounds, Robert Skerrett 2,325 pounds, John Kirwan 1,212 pounds, Patrick Blake 10,000 pounds, Martin French lost 1,500 pounds, Thomas Blake 909 pounds and David Bodkin lost 824 pounds.

A tax assessment of the town of Plymouth at the end of 1719 shows that the houses taxed for the whole town was 373 pounds. Individual people's houses were also assessed. William Gerrish's house was valued at 50 pounds, Martin French's 25 pounds, John Lynch, John Blake, John Kirwan and George French's were valued at 15 pounds.

By 1729, the thirty largest landowners on Montserrat had controlled 80 percent of the total land and owned 60 percent of the slaves, three-quarters of the sugar mills and the majority of the livestock.

By 1720, Irish people had held upper positions or gone elsewhere and there were only 95 Irish indentured servants. As most Irish households on Montserrat owned slaves, they were not working in the field but involved with the implementation and maintenance of the slave economy and trade. By the full abolition of slavery in 1838, Irish links with the British West Indies were mostly over. When the emancipation of the slaves reached Montserrat, many African slaves became Catholics following their owners' faith. Between 1824 and 1828, the Rev. Father O'Hannan baptised hundreds of slaves.

Buying land

There were some drives for Irish people to come and stay on the island. They were able to buy land on Montserrat relatively easily. Despite the fact that various laws against Irish Catholics existed, there were not strictly applied. According to a list of 30 large sugar planters in 1729, the largest landowner on Montserrat was an Englishman George Wyke, but the rest of the top five landowners were all Irish people. Then comes a Catholic Farrell, then, the Trants, the Whites and the Roaches, each owned between 300 and 370 acres of land, up to 225 slaves, and two or more sugar mills apiece. The Lynches possessed 121 slaves and 360 acres of land. The Darcys had 123 slaves and 350 acres of land. According to the list, more than two-thirds were dominated by Irish surnames.

Troublemakers

Life in the early tropical colony was tough and brutal. With hundreds of thousands forced or unwillingly transported people, there was constantly bickering. Irish people in Montserrat often got into trouble with other people which turned into violent affairs. An observer described how the people from the British Isles were perceived: 'And whereas also there are several persons of his Majesty's subjects of his three nations, that is to say, England, Scotland and Ireland, residing in the Island, and oftentimes as well in Drink as sober...certain words of distinction do arise between his Majesty's subjects of the said three nations...as English Dog, Scott's Dog, Tory, Irish Dog, Cavalier, and Roundhead, and many other opprobrious, scandalous, and disgraceful terms, the Breech of his Majesty's Peace etc. and by certain Quaralls that may arise by reason of such ill language... to the endangering the loss of the lives of many of his Majesty's good subjects of the Three Nations'.[76]

Culture

Montserrat is dubbed as Ireland's only colony or the emerald isle of the Caribbean. A term 'the Irish Imperialism' is used specifically for Montserrat. Its regional flag depicts Erin, the female symbol of Ireland, holding a harp alongside the Union Jack, as it is still officially a British Overseas Territory. The shamrock has been the island's symbol, the emblem on its flag and its official passport validation stamp. On the door of the Governor's house, a shamrock is carved. According to Anthropologist John C. Messenger, there were 12 Irish influences in Montserrat: ubiquitous place names; Irish-derived family names; language inheritance; oral art such as storytelling; musical styles; dance styles; pieces of ancient mythology; codes of etiquette and hospitality; illegal distilling and drinking; specific foods; motor pattern; and systems of values. Many Irish derived surnames and place names can be seen throughout the island. St. Patrick's Day on 17 March in Montserrat is a national holiday to honour its Irish heritage, and also an attempted slave rebellion occurred on this day in 1768. Irish surnames were chosen by African slaves at emancipation, not for any love of the Irish, because at that time Irish slave owners predominated on the island and 'these surnames indicate a particularly nasty form of human exploitation, slavery', according to Akenson.[77] In Montserrat, more than 30 percent of the surnames of the black residents are Irish, some of the common names are Sweeney, Riley, O'Brien and Kelly. The traditional musical instruments on the island are the fife and drum just like the Irish bodhran; one of the folk dances called heel and toe, bears a similarity to the jig; the national dish 'goat water' probably derives from the

Connemara stew. Humphrey O'Sullivan wrote in his diary on 1 April 1831: 'I hear that Irish is the mother tongue in Montserrat... since the time of Cromwell who transported some Irish people... Irish is spoken commonly there by both whites and blacks'. W.F. Butler wrote a letter from Cork on 27 June 1905, quoting a Mr. C. Cremen from Cork Harbour Commissioners' Office: 'There is an old saying among our Cork sailors of the old sailing-vessel days, 'In Montserrat, where the blacks speak Irish'.

Antigua

It was also Christopher Columbus who named the island during his 1493 voyage. Antigua looks perfect for agriculture as it is mostly flat with a few gentle hills and a highly indented coastline. But there is no river on the island. Emanuel Bowen, an English map engraver who was working on his map of Antigua in 1750 wrote: 'In times of drouth (sic) when all their ponds are dry, and their cisterns almost empty, they are obliged to fetch their fresh water from Montserrat'. An Englishman Christopher Codrington and some English people in St Christopher first moved to Antigua to develop a settlement in 1632. Because Codrington initially came from Barbados, he brought with him sugar technology and successfully developed the island as a sugar colony. Then, 100 more settlers from London came to settle in Barbuda, a nearby island.

Irish settlers on Antigua did well, too. Quite a few of them ended up becoming wealthy planters and merchants. Nicholas Lynch was one of the most successful Irish planters in Antigua. Another high profile Irish man who was also a merchant and planter in Barbados and Montserrat was John Blake. When he died, his land was passed to his daughter, Catharine Blake. The first Bodkin to arrive in Antigua was Dominick. According to his will dated 9 October 1674, he left monies and items to various Catholic orders including the Benedictines, Augustines of Gallaway, the Franciscans and Dominicans. He also mentioned his relatives in Galway. He was a Catholic but all family baptisms, marriages and burials are recorded in the Anglican registers. Peter Gaynor from Ireland was a planter and merchant. Upon his death in 1738, his substantial fortune of approximately 200,000 pounds was inherited by his son-in-law Sir George Colebrook, Chairman of the East India Company, member of Parliament and a London banker. Samuel Martin was born in Antigua in 1693. The land that his royalist grandfather possessed in Ulster was confiscated by Cromwell's army and he fled to the West Indies. Samuel's father developed a large plantation in Antigua but was killed by his slaves. Samuel was still small at that time and sent to Ireland. After getting married, he returned to Antigua. He had many family connections in Ireland which included his cousin George Martin, a politically influential merchant in Dublin.

Jamaica

The island of Jamaica was inhabited by the Taino tribes prior to the arrival of Christopher Columbus in 1494 who famously described it as 'the fairest isle'. When the Spanish took control of Jamaica, they enslaved the Tainos but almost the entire population had become extinct by 1600 due to various conflicts and foreign diseases. Subsequently, the Spanish brought hundreds of enslaved Africans to Jamaica but Spain used the island mainly as a military base to supply colonising efforts in the mainland Americas.

Western Design

Politically, Irish Catholics always played a crucial role in the Caribbean. Oliver Cromwell launched his Western Design, an imperial policy to break the Spanish monopoly of the Caribbean and to conquer the Spanish West Indies in April 1655, and focused on the conquest of Hispaniola (currently the Dominican Republic occupies 64% of the island while Haiti the rest 36%). The English attacked Santo Domingo with approximately 7,000 soldiers or some estimates up to 8,200 and 120 cavalry units but it failed to seize it. It was Don Juan Morfo Geraldino y Burco, or John Murphy Fitzgerald Burke, a soldier from Galway, that led the local Spanish force to victory after deserting the French and English buccaneers of Tortuga (Haiti). But attacking Santo Domingo turned out to be disastrous. The dead and wounded were estimated to be more than 1,600 and the remaining troops were not willing to continue the battle so the English decided to move on to a less populated and poorly defended island, Jamaica.

Located in the middle of the Caribbean Sea, Jamaica was in an ideal location for striking against Spanish ships and raids on Hispaniola, Cuba and Central America. Because the English aimed at securing a permanent base of military operations in the Caribbean, Cromwell sent the fleet into Kingston Harbour as part of his Western Design. Jamaica was founded through bloody battles from its inception. An English force led by Admiral Sir William Penn and General Robert Venables of several thousand soldiers contained an overwhelming number of Irish men, arrived from Ireland, Barbados, St Christopher or elsewhere when the population of Jamaica was only around 2,500. Irish indentured servants who were recruited to join the armed forces were called cabbage stalk soldiers as they were armed with their cabbage stalk pikes.

Their mission was successful but the excitement of the conquest of Jamaica instantly diminished as the soldiers struggled to survive. Because the invasion occurred at the beginning of the rainy season, mosquito-borne diseases took countless lives. Within three weeks, it is estimated around 3,000 men were sick, dying or dead. By November, only about 3,700 troops of the initial invasion force remained alive. After a few months of conquest, it looked more like defeat as an incoming army commander observed: 'The soldiery many dead, their carcasses lying unburied in the high-ways, and amongst bushes'.

He witnessed that many of them that were alive, walked like ghosts or dead men: 'As I went through the town, lay groaning and crying out, bread for the Lord's sake. The truth is, when I set my foot first on land, I saw nothing but symptoms of necessity and desolation'.[78] Nevertheless, officials encouraged the remaining soldiers to develop farms and plantations. They promised to bring 'poor maids' from Ireland to provide wives for them. The island remained more of a military camp rather than an agricultural settlement in the first few years.

Migration to Jamaica

The demand for labour on the plantations in the newly acquired land prompted not just prisoners of war but led to mass kidnappings in Ireland. According to a pamphlet published in 1660, the governor of Galway was grabbing any Irish people he could find: 'It was a usual practice with Colonel Strubber, the governor of Galway, and other commanders in the said county, to take people out of their beds at night and sell them for slaves to the Indies, and by computation sold out of the said county about a thousand souls'.[79] Cromwell appointed his son Henry in 1655 to deal with the internal divisions in the army in Ireland. Henry suggested transporting 1,500 disbanded soldiers in Ireland to Jamaica as planters and to secure 1,000 young Irish girls, or as Secretary Thurloe called them 'Irish wenches'. Henry answered that there would be no difficulty, 'Only that force must be used in taking them,' and he suggested up to 2,000 boys from 12- to 14-years-old could be seized and shipped there because 'Who knows but it might be a means to make them Englishmen – I mean Christians?' In the end, the Council voted that 1,000 boys aged from 12, young men and an equal number of girls be transported from Ireland: the boys as bondmen and the girls to serve these soldiers in Jamaica. What's more, the existing Tudor law allowed a plethora of vagrants from Ireland to transport. The English authorities ultimately viewed the forcible removal of Irish people as a mercy. Henry was in favour of transportation rather than executions.

England was committed to develop its newly acquired colony. Oliver Cromwell, with help from his son Henry, issued a proclamation to encourage trade and settlement by exempting the inhabitants from taxes. Jamaican goods were free of custom for seven years. Planters in Barbados also moved to Jamaica as they lost their workers who were recruited as soldiers. There were some incentives for freemen as they were given 30 acres of land and tools upon settling in Jamaica. In 1662, the second governor Lord Thomas Windsor brought a proclamation from the King giving Jamaica's non-slave population the rights of English citizens. He laid the foundations of a local governing system such as a crown-appointed governor acting with the advice of a nominated council in the legislature.

The appointment of Thomas Modyford, a notable planter in Barbados, as governor in 1664 transformed the island into a prosperous colony. He brought not just his extensive experience and knowledge but 1,000 colonists and settlers who were mainly small planters. They owned slaves but had limited prospects in Barbados as there was a shortage of land. In a sense, those who couldn't own decent land in Barbados were given a second chance in Jamaica where they were able to obtain land, wealth, status and freedom. Modyford served his adopted island efficiently but there was a big obstacle to agricultural expansion. A significant part of Jamaica's economy was formed from privateering from the beginning. Early settlers were described as rather 'looser sorts' who were good at 'plundering rather than planting'. Modyford had orders to rein in the privateers when he was appointed governor but given the circumstances, he strongly believed it was more profitable to cooperate with them. He authorised missions against the Spanish and other enemies and received his percentage of goods seized at sea. It was the height of piracy during the 1660s and a score of pirates, including

Henry Morgan, a former indentured servant in Barbados, were operating from Port Royal.

Settlers, particularly with money, acquired large tracts, imported slaves, started sugar and other colonial trades and promptly settled comfortably. At one point in the 17th century, two thirds of the white population were Irish. From 1671 to 1675, approximately 500 Irish Catholics were transported to Jamaica via Bristol. The largest British West Indian island quickly became a so-called dumping ground for the Irish Catholics with 'insolent behaviour'. Between 1671 and 1679, out of an annual average of about 700 whites, half were indentured servants. According to the estimate of 1675, Bristol ships calling in Irish ports for provisions brought 500 servants with three or four indentured years.

About 1,200 or 1,400 freemen, freewomen and indentured servants arrived in Jamaica from England each year. But a quarter of them did not remain in Jamaica. Some historians estimate that out of the 10,000 Irish servants that left Barbados in the last quarter of the 17th century, half of them arrived in Jamaica where plenty of land was still available for small farmers. Many Irish settlers lived near the internal frontier close to the Maroons. The German/Jewish migration was also numerous, second in volume to the Irish. By 1673, Jamaica already had more than 9,500 slaves which was more than all Leeward Islands combined. It was in 1689 when the numbers of white servants started decreasing.

Until 1700, there was a constant flow of Irish indentured servants from English and Irish ports such as Kinsale, Cork, Galway and Bristol. And there was a huge influx of Irish servants in 1728. The 1730 census recorded 2,171 masters, 3,993 servants, 1,484 white children and 74,525 African slaves as living in Jamaica. Irish people from Ireland and elsewhere continuously arrived until 1841. By the 19th century, first hand observations were recorded by former Irish residents of Jamaica who returned to Europe.

Problematic newcomers

On every occasion, the English regretted the mass arrival of Irish Catholics in their colonies even though they were necessary. By 1799, a plethora of exiled United Irishmen had joined the maroon colonies. A letter to the Rev. William Miller of Sixmilebridge, Clare from his sister in Jamaica reveals that Irish residents were the cause of great concern: 'A vast number of United Irishmen, transported from this kingdom, have been landed there and incautiously drafted into the regiments. As soon as they got arms into their hands, they deserted, and fled into the mountains, where they have been joined by large bodies of the natives and such of the French as were in the island. There have already been some engagements between this party and the King's troops; several have been killed and wounded on both sides'.[80] Because there were simply too many troublemakers, Governor Robert Hunter complained that such 'great numbers' had arrived during the preceding decade that 'the servants and lower rank of people in Jamaica chiefly consisted of Irish Papists'.[81] Hunter remarked that the indentured servants in Jamaica were mostly Irish Catholics who were a danger to the island and their introduction should be restrained. He also warned in 1731 that the large influx of Irish Catholics was infiltrating the government.

The Benefit of being white

The newly arrived Irish people from other British West Indian colonies were more eager to benefit from their whiteness in an expanding economy. Catholic discrimination was not extremely severe in Jamaica as the top priority of England was to develop the island. In a relatively short period of time, average Irish people climbed up the social ladder and reached the rank of middling planter. By 1670, there had been 717 property-holders and more than 10 percent were Irish people and quite a few Irish people were owners of slaves.

Affluent Lynch merchants were also conducting all kinds

of profitable businesses in Jamaica. Like on other Leeward Islands, former Irish indentured servants did very well within their lifetime, in other words, they led a comfortable life within 10 years after they became free. Just like Montserrat, their assimilation into the British system was especially quick in Jamaica. Although it is impossible to know who were actually Irish, Scottish or English, according to inventory records and property maps, Irish surnames were scattered all over the island and land was granted to the people with Irish surnames. One of them who started off as a humble labourer is Teague Mackmarroe (or Tadhg MacMorrough). He owned eight slaves and became a so-called middling planter. By the time Cornelius O'Brien died on 29 May, 1759 in St Thomas, he had owned 32 male and 22 female slaves, 16 boys and girls (he named one of the boys 'Good-boy' and the girls 'Hope'), horses, cows, sheep, tables, pictures, chests, books, and a plantation, a total of 3,472 pounds which was a substantial amount of money in those days.

Wealthy people who lost properties due to the Cromwellian conquest arrived on the same ship with indentured servants. The affluent Hooke family escaped to the British West Indies after Cromwellian soldiers attacked Hooke Castle in Wexford. Upon arriving, Hooke served as Assistant to the Commissary General of Musters in Jamaica. A shortage of legal personnel in Jamaica was filled thanks to gentry families from Munster and Connacht. The names recorded during the compensation hearings in 1837 included O'Connor, O'Hara, Talbot, Martin, Hennessy, Burke, O'Sullivan, Boyle, Tierney, Geoghagan, Dillon, Walsh and O'Meally. The Kellys of Lisduff and the Galways literally founded the judicial tradition in Jamaica. Edmond Kelly became attorney general of Jamaica in the 1720s, and he appointed his brother Denis its chief justice in the 1740s. By that time, the Kellys had dominated the Jamaican judicial system. Denis inherited the Lisduff estate, hence he earned his nickname 'Jamaica Kelly'. In 1752, his daughter and heiress,

Elizabeth married into the Browne family of Westport, County Mayo. Just like all wealthy Irish people, such as the Brownes and the Kellys, they increased their wealth by swiftly adapting to changes particularly, religion. Elizabeth Kelly's wealth was substantial which made the Brownes Ireland's premier absentee plantation owners in the British West Indies. Just like Britain created the absentee landlord system in Ireland, absentee planters commonly existed throughout the British West Indies. Prestigious Irish people promptly formed the ruling class of Jamaica. Howe Peter Browne, second Marquess of Sligo (1788-1845) was a governor of Jamaica from 1834 to 1836. Dowell O'Reilly (1795-1855) was attorney general of Jamaica from 1831 to 1855, Richard Robert Madden (1798-1886) was a special magistrate in Jamaica and wrote a book about his experience in *A Twelvemonth's Residence in the West Indies, During the Transition from Slavery to Apprenticeship* (1835). In 1810, when Andrew M'Kenzie from County Down, a vernacular poet published his *Poems and Songs on Different Subjects in Belfast*, more than 45 of his subscribers were from Jamaica.

Irish governors

There were some high profile officials, both Irish or of descent, often with remarkable army careers. William O'Brien (or Brayne) was military governor of Jamaica (1656-1657), the son of the 1st Earl of Inchiquin. He served under his father in various military activities in France and Spain. William was a Privy Councillor and Captain General of the Forces in Algeria. Born in Kilmallock, Limerick, Eyre Coote served as governor of Jamaica (1806-8). He had a long and significant career in the British Army which included the American War of Independence and the French Revolutionary Wars. His nephew (same name) was also a significant officer, Sir Eyre Coote, who was the celebrated Indian General. John Keane was the son of Sir John Keane 1st Baronet and was born in Belmont, Offaly. Since joining the British Army at the age of 11, he rose to the rank of Lieutenant Colonel. He governed Jamaica from 1827 to 1829.

After emancipation

Plantation and slave owners typically received compensation after emancipation of slavery. In Jamaica, the Earl of Sligo received approximately 5,526 pounds for owning 286 slaves. There is a long list of Irish names who received compensation: Brigit Garvey, Elizabeth Anne Carroll, Jane Welch, Elizabeth Geoghegan, Anne O'Meally, Eleanor Tierney, Elizabeth Anne Sherlocke, Elizabeth Sleven, Mary O'Sullivan, Rebecca Fergus, Elizabeth Burke, Cecilia Jane Murphy, Mary Anne Connolly, Ann Rattigan, Mary Anne B. Hennessey, Jane Boyle, Brigit Dillion and Mary Curtin, to name a few. After the abolition of slavery in 1834, the House of Assembly offered a bounty for the importation of white immigrants. The Irish were still arriving to boost the labour force, albeit on a much smaller scale. They mainly worked on sugar and coffee plantations as skilled workers and they were also valued in the police force. On 28 February 1841, 127 newcomers whose professions include tailor, servant, labourer, carpenter, barber and wheelwright arrived from Limerick, one of the last ships from Limerick to Kingston, aboard the SS *Robert Kerr*. Many included the whole family with small children. The voyage from Ireland took seven weeks: 'They were brought away with difficulty, for O'Connell denounced the emigration scheme with all his vigour, declaring it to be nothing else but a system of white slavery - a new wrong inflicted upon suffering Ireland by the Saxon race. The ship while in the Irish port, was guarded night and day by the police: only one-third of the number she was intended to carry sailed in her, and no steam-tug would venture to tow her out of the harbour'.[82] *The Kingston Gleaner*, one of the oldest newspapers in Jamaica, also wrote that Irish emigrants landed in Kingston 'wearing their best clothes and temperance medals'. The year 1841 marked the end of large scale Irish immigration to Jamaica.

The Bahamas

The first permanent colony in the Bahamas was established on the island of Eleuthera in 1648 when 70 English Puritans settlers mainly from Bermuda arrived. According to the list of the early settlers of the Bahamas, amongst them included a large number of Irish sounding names such as Kelly, Kerr, Brown and Cochran. As the thin soil was not suitable for agriculture, only a few settlers remained on Eleuthera and started looting occasional shipwrecks.

After they arrived, they found work but often 'returned to their old courses'. They started bothering local people and many were prosecuted for 'different felonies' by the Attorney-General and shipped to the North American mainland. There was a baker in Nassau who had an Irish apprentice called Thomas Flynn. There was a person called Thomas Glynn in the arrest warrant. In the end, the confused authority arrested both of them and deported them off of the island. Quite a few Irish vagrants settled in New Providence and Irish poor whites were also living on the island from the early period. In order to make a living, they cooperated with enslaved women and joined the so-called 'huckstering trade'. They copied their methods of bartering, selling and distributing. The most common items were drinks, poultry and stock.

Because of the Treaty of Versailles in 1783, Florida and Cuba were ceded by thc English to the Spanish in exchange for the Bahamas. Quite a few loyalists also ended up there, established plantations and accumulated wealth. For instance, John O'Halloran eventually owned nine slaves and became postmaster and a member of the Assembly; Henry Glenton was a small planter and provost with six slaves and a small vessel; John Jordan, an Irish native became Director of Ironworks in the Abaco islands. The bulk of the population settled on New

Providence Island.

Saint Lucia

Governor Francis Lord Willoughby requested he colonise Saint Lucia and King Charles II accepted it in 1664. Thomas Warner, the son of the governor of St Christopher Sir Thomas Warner, claimed the island for England. Governor Willoughby recruited 1,300 freeman and small planters from Barbados. The large majority of them were Irish but killed by the Carib, local indigenous people and disease.

Tortola

The earliest records referring to the presence of slaves was in 1665. The British removed 67 slaves from Bermuda and brought them to Tortola. The mass importation of slave labour started in the mid-1750s when sugar production started. According to the 1717 census of Tortola, when putting the percentage of the places of birth for heads of household, the total of British and Irish households was at 30%.[83] Quite a few people who were 'banished' ended up in here.

British Guiana

The Blair brothers, James and Lambert from Newry, moved to Saint Eustatia (Eustatius) in the late 18th century. According to their 1790 accounts, the largest items of purchase were slaves for their client Mr. Stevenson. They invested in the new colony Demerara (British Guiana) in 1803 when Britain took it from the Netherlands. They established a large sugar plantation called Blairmont. After emancipation, plantation owners received compensation. With 1,598 slaves, James' son received one of the highest amounts within the British Empire – 83,530 pounds 8 shillings and 11 pence. Both James and Lambert married the Stopfords of Courtown, County Wexford.

The Halls from Ramelton, Donegal initially established

themselves in Barbados but swiftly moved to invest in the newly acquired Guiana. With the wealth they accumulated in Barbados, they became absentee planters there. The McGarel brothers, Charles, Peter and John, from Larne, Antrim arrived before 1808. The sons of a local innkeeper or cobbler, they became partners in the local merchant firm of Johnson, Dyett, McGarel and Co., of Stabroek (changed to Georgetown after 1812). They were involved with importing supplies and consumer goods from Britain for sale to local residents. By 1820, Charles had moved to London. His firm of Hall McGarel functioned as a London agent for estates in British Guiana. In the 1830s, the partners in Hall McGarel were major beneficiaries of slave compensation, receiving almost 100,000 pounds for about 2,500 slaves. The partners' dealings with plantations in the colony brought more compensation. Charles McGarel had enough money to purchase land and an estate at Magheramorne near Larne in 1842. His philanthropic activities included funding of the national school system in Larne, building the Town Hall, a cemetery and almshouses.

Saint Croix

The Danish king acquired this island from France in 1733. But his people showed no interest in developing the island. Free from mistrust by the British establishment, many seasoned Irish merchants and planters from nearby islands arrived. They were well-established Galway merchant families, Theobald Bourke, John Skerrett, Laurence Bodkin, Henry Ryan, John Baker, Mathias Farrall, Nicholas Tuite, the Kirwans, the Husseys and the Blakes who started using Saint Croix as a base for their trading business as they smuggled slaves to Saint-Domingue (currently part of Haiti) and loaded up with sugar to sell in Europe, particularly London. The fact that the Irish had already developed a highly sophisticated mercantile community in the British capital, the hub of the international sugar trade, made them easily to conduct their trade. Laurence Bodkin had imported a substantial number of Africans to Saint Croix from various locations by 1760. The Tuites and the Ryans also did a brisk business by inter-island trading with Saint Croix.

By 1747, many Irish merchants and planters with good kinship networks had bought land in Saint Croix and become extremely prosperous. During the height of the Seven Years' War from 1756 to 1763, the Irish in Saint Croix were responsible for 30 percent of Danish sugar exports. One of the most notable residents was Nicholas Tuite (1705-72) who was born on Montserrat where he possessed 100 acres and 41 slaves in St. Patrick's parish. Later, he came to live on Saint Croix in his thirties. He was the owner of seven plantations and part-owner of seven others. He built a Catholic church in the capital, Christiansted. Gaelic speaking Father Dominic Allen first served here and a second Dominican Hyacinth Kennedy was sent from Ireland to live on a Tuite plantation where he baptised 150 slaves. 20 years later, Tuite moved to settle in London. He acted as an agent for those who remained in the West Indies and as an advisor to the Danes on their mercantile interests. The Danish king declared him as the founder of Saint Croix and made him a chancellor, granting him Danish citizenship in 1760. In 1749, he settled in London and bought Sion House.

Cuba

Historically and traditionally, Ireland and Spain had been always close allies. In fact, some of the early settlers of Ireland came from Spain. And in 1588, the survivors of the Spanish Armada settled in Ireland. During the 17th century, the clashes between Protestants and Catholics in Ireland prompted a mass emigration of Irish people to Spain. After the defeat of James II of England and the Catholics in Ireland, several thousand Irish followers of the King left the country and joined the armies of various European countries. Spain maintained four regiments composed entirely of Irishmen with their own uniform and Irish officers for a long time. The majority of them also served in the Spanish overseas territories.

By the time the villa of San Cristobal de la Habana was founded in 1519, quite a few Irish people had already been living, serving as seamen, generals and soldiers enlisted in the Spanish Navy. Some of the most significant generals were O'Reilly, O'Donnell, O'Farrill and O'Gaban. They were also involved with liberation wars on both sides throughout the Spanish colonies.

In 1665, Juan Duany whose father was from Sligo arrived in Santiago de Cuba to take part in the fortification work. Throughout the 18th century, people with the surname Duany held office as council members and mayors in Cuba. Quite a few slave merchants originally from Ireland or of Irish descent were also based in Cuba. After the Treaty of Utrecht in 1713, Britain had the right to supply slaves to the Spanish colonies. Ricardo O'Farrill, or Richard Farrell, who was born in Montserrat to parents from Longford acquired the position in Havana. He ended up becoming a considerable slave dealer and his descendants all became substantial planters in Cuba. Ricardo O'Farrill and Wergent Nicholson ran a company and in their Santiago de Cuba branch, Mr. Cumberlege and Mr. Walsh were based. Ricardo O'Farrill had a Spanish wife and they established a prominent family in the development of the country and also at the heart of the Spanish-Cuban aristocracy. The surname O'Farrill appears in the family trees of almost all the Havana families with noble titles.

Just like in British colonies, Irish people also worked as indentured servants in various sugar plantations such as in Cuba and the Canary Islands. This means that Irish merchants were always present in the Spanish colonial system. Consequently, Irish settlers had a huge influence on the economic, political and cultural development of Cuba. In 1817, there was the first proper Irish settlement in Cuba. In December 1835, more than 300 Irish people who had been contracted in New York arrived in Havana to work as railroad workers. The construction of the island's first railway from Havana to Guines from 1835 to 1838, was highly dangerous and the sugar railroad claimed many lives. On top of their labour, they were also used as a whitening agent on the island's black population, according to the Hispano-Cuban colonisation policy. The best example of this policy is in Argentina which was considered a great success as it largely diminished its Afro-Argentine and indigenous populations by these means and Irish people were part of it, too. In the British Empire, however, the British didn't take this obvious whitening policy seriously, although a clandestine breeding policy existed.

Puerto Rico

In the late 1770s when Puerto Rico was developing commercial agriculture, a large number of Irish people arrived to settle as planters such as Felipe Doran from Carlow, Miguel Conway, Patricio Fitzpatrick, Jaime Kiernan, Antonio Skerret, Tomas O'Daly, Juan Nagle, amongst others. Most of them owned thriving sugar haciendas. Irish people were also involved with the tobacco industry. The Quinlans and the Conroys were also notable tobacco traders. High profile military officers from Ireland customary existed such as Alejandro O'Reilly, Tomas O'Daly, Timoteo O'Daly, Pedro O'Daly and Arturo O'Neill. Because of cordial military ties with Spain, Irishmen who joined the Spanish armed forces such as the Hibernia Infantry Regiment in Spain moved to the New World with them and put down roots.

Although it was not strictly observed, Spain banned foreigners from conducting commercial trade on their soil. Juan Tuite was a resident of Saint Croix, partaking in various businesses with London and the Americas. In 1776, he proposed setting up an Irish colony of 100 families in Puerto Rico and asked for authorisation to bring in provisions, tools and slaves. But his proposition was rejected.

Hispaniola

During the European colonial days, the island of Hispaniola (current Haiti and the Dominican Republic) was called Saint Domingue (French), Santo Domingo (Spanish) or sometimes the entire island had also been referred to as Haiti. The Irish who had a strong link to France arrived in Saint Domingue. John Stapleton and his wife Helen Skerret became planters in Saint Domingue. They left Ireland for the French colony in the 17th century and they were later ennobled by the French Crown. With the fortune they made, they purchased a property in Nantes. The Butlers who were based in La Rochelle, France sent their two sons to Saint Domingue to establish plantations. Philip Walsh, a Waterford merchant, settled in Saint Malo, France in 1685. His son Antoine Walsh was a successful slave trader. His ships transported at least 12,000 slaves from 1730 to 1753. Those Irish slave merchants who accumulated wealth bought castles (chateaux) in France and established the Irish college in Nantes. The Walshes also had their regiment in the Irish brigade. Subsequently, they invested their wealth in the Caribbean. In Saint Domingue, wealthy Irish settlers included: the Walshes, the Stapletons, the Skerrets, the Butlers, the Sheils, the O'Gormans, the Rourkes, the Macnamaras and the Plunkets. There were plenty of 'grands blancs' but there were also 'petits blancs' who were small holders, overseers, shopkeepers and small scale merchants.

Guadeloupe/ Martinique

Because Ireland had a close relationship with France, Irish people had been seen throughout the French colonies. Irish merchants imported slaves and provisions from Ireland to the French islands of Guadeloupe and Martinique. By the 1670s, there had been 200 Irish people on Guadeloupe who were living 'much as they do at home in little huts, planting potatoes and tobacco, and as much indigo as will buy them canvas and brandy and never advance so far as sugar planting'.[84] Britain captured this sugar island a couple of times from France. William Burke was appointed as Secretary for Guadeloupe in 1759, but shortly the island was returned to France. On Martinique, the Kirwans, the Roches, the Lynches and the Skerrets were also amassing wealth as quite a few Irish merchants played a notable role in the French slave trade.

Chapter 4

Colonialism in question

The British colonisation of Ireland created the Irish Diaspora. Britain may have treated Ireland as a subordinate, but in reality their relationship occasionally looked more like an equal partnership in the Caribbean. Ultimately, the Irish were seen as the enemy within. At one point, the Irish in the Caribbean were highly visible in all social classes. There is no doubt that they have left a long-lasting legacy on both sides of the Atlantic. But how does it look when this neglected Irish story is located in the British context? First of all, were they actually sent to the Caribbean as slaves? What role did they actually play in the context of the British Empire? Did they influence in any way the end of slavery?

Were Irish people slaves?

Between the 17th and the early 18th centuries, tens of thousands of people from the British Isles crossed the Atlantic mainly as indentured servants. Because Ireland was fighting against England, a substantial number of Irish men were captured by the English and put in jail. Estimates vary but more than 10,000 people who escaped execution especially during the turbulent civil war period were transported straight from various jails in Ireland in handcuffs. They didn't sign indenture agreements or contracts. In fact, it is impossible to know what percentage of labour was forced, involuntary or voluntary, or what their lives looked like. Actual indentured servants didn't write down their own experiences because early labourers were often illiterate or had no means to write and tell their stories. However, quite a few visitors such as medical doctors, merchants and Catholic priests observed how they actually lived and worked in the

Caribbean. For example, Thomas Povey, an English merchant with extensive British West Indian investments wrote in 1658 that the majority of Irish servants in Barbados and St Christopher had been transported by the English state for treason. John Scott, an English adventurer, visited the British West Indies and witnessed Irish servants working in fields without stockings under the scorching sun: 'They were derided by the negroes, and branded with the Epithet of white slaves'.

Were Irish people actually slaves or servants? As might be expected, recently the term 'Irish slave myth' has become one of the most popular internet search topics in order to debunk the myth of whether the Irish were really slaves and/or black. The memes typically claim: 'The Irish were slaves, too. We got over it, so why can't you?' or 'The enslavement of Africans was not such a big deal because white people were slaves, too'. People from diverse backgrounds started using this term with various connotations which include the unfair treatment that immigrants have been receiving in certain localities as well as to counter the historical burden of African slavery and the Black Lives Matter movement, not to mention the rise of nationalism and populist movements in recent years on both sides of the Atlantic which are also pushing the subject. There has been much controversy over the descriptions of Irish workers who were transported to the British colonies in the New World. There is no denying that Irish and African people shared a similar history in the context of the Caribbean and to some degree in mainland America. But first of all, what is the difference between slave and servant?

Terminology

A servant, or an indentured servant, to be precise in this context, came to work in the British colonies for a limited period of time, normally a few years or up to seven years in exchange for passage, board, lodging and freedom dues. On the other hand, a slave is a person who is the legal property of another person.

Once you are a slave, you are owned, you are enslaved for life. If a parent is a slave, his/her child is also a slave at birth. (In some cases, when a father was a wealthy European planter, his child was able to get good education.) So the obvious difference is whether one can be set free in the future or not.

For example, a historian Hilary Beckles wrote in his book *White Servitude and Black Slavery in Barbados, 1627-1715*: 'In Barbados indentured servants were temporary chattels, though we do not argue that they were slaves in the sense that blacks were. Irish people were called black men in white skins. Indentured servants had fixed terms while black slaves were owned for life, although some servants were treated atrociously like black slaves'. According to Abbot Emerson Smith, who wrote *Colonists in Bondage: White Servitude and Convict Labor in America, 1607-1776*: 'There is no evidence of whites serving in perpetual servitude'. By the 1640s, laws had been set up to differentiate between the servant (Europeans) and the enslaved (African people). Under colonial law, bonded Europeans were called indentured servants. Indentured servants had first and family names, whereas the slaves had no names (in the colonisers' eyes) and treated as livestock as they were measured in monetary value. Indentured servants were considered legally human, while slaves were not. Indentured servants were sometimes referred as 'stock', while slaves were 'commodities'. According to Richard Ligon who lived in Barbados and wrote a book *A True and Exact History of the Island of Barbados,* the slaves were 'bred along with the horses and cattle'. In most cases, servants were treated better than slaves because there was a law to protect them. Irish servants had a higher social status than African slaves.

Four types of indentured servants

There were roughly four main types of Irish indentured labourers: free-willers/redemptioners; involuntary labourers; child labourers; and forced servants such as political prisoners and convicts. Free-willer or voluntary indentured servants normally signed a contract. The period could be around four years. Often with skills and education, they normally made a contract of indenture. Involuntary servants included vagrants and widows with no means of survival who had no choice but to leave. They were unwilling or forced labourers who were typically sold for cash on arrival. The period could be up to seven years, but this was not strictly promised. Child labourers could be orphans or vagrants. Spiriters were those who were kidnapped or abducted while asleep or on the street. Convict servants, whose labour was bought and sold without their consent, didn't sign a contract and they were treated atrociously. They were forcefully transported to the British West Indies without knowing a specific period of servitude, where they were going to or what would happen to them. Upon arriving, the master purchased their labour for a certain period of time, depending on their age, convictions, professions and skills, according to law. In many cases, they worked indefinitely as they died before their indenture was expired.

Legal difference between slaves and servants

By law, indentured servants had rights and they were not owned for life, unlike African slaves. Considering forced indentured servants and African slaves' short lifespan, they were both forced, unfree, suffered from brutal treatment and harsh working and living conditions. But servants had more rights that slaves didn't have. Although servants equally suffered from terrible living and working conditions, and various maltreatments, they didn't get killed for a punishment unlike the way in which African slaves were tortured or killed on a regular basis. For instance, two landowners, Sweeny and Lynch, saw Andrew Lynch sued for 'trespass...to beat, wound, ill treat a negro man slave named Sampson the property of the said Edmund Sweeny so that thereof the said slave died'. This wasn't an uncommon isolated incident. The killing of an African slave was a crime of property and it was not of interest to a higher court so the case was held in a lower court. But it was always dropped without any sanction of the defendant. If an Irish servant witnessed an African slave stealing, he was able to kill the slave legally and was rewarded with sugar. The owner of the slave could purchase another slave with public money. If enslaved Africans assaulted any white Christian, they were severely tortured, maimed and often killed. Conspiratorial slaves were legally burned alive, beheaded, gibbeted and castrated.

In principle, the indentured labourers or bondsmen might not be classified as slavery as they were legally treated differently but this fact doesn't mean servants necessarily had better treatment. According to Richard Ligon who wrote a book on his first-hand account, Barbados was divided into three types of people – masters, servants and slaves. 'The slaves and their posterity, being subject to their masters forever, are kept and preserv'd with greater care than the servants, who are theirs but for five years, according of the law of the island. So that for the time, the servants have the worser lives, for they are put to very hard labour, ill lodging, and their dyet very sleight'. As legal property, slaves were subject to their masters until they died, therefore they were kept with greater care than the servants who worked for a specific time period. This was basically the law throughout the British West Indies. The servant's indenture was considered legal property. So their remaining time could be legally left in wills, traded for commodities and sold. Because their labour meant their lives, the servants in Barbados were treated as somewhat like a commodity during their indentured period, not for life.

Another difference was that there were breeding rules in the British West Indies. The slaves were encouraged to have babies which would only increase their value as property, while the servants were not as it was costly from a masters' point of view.

Another common practice was that European colonisers often captured and stole African slaves from the enemy territories.

Some researchers and historians describe Irish workers during this period as slaves. In a legal sense, Europeans were never slaves but it was true that some Irish political prisoners and convicts were servants for life without indentures. For instance, Sean O'Callaghan, the author of *To Hell or Barbados: The Ethnic Cleansing of Ireland,* somewhat differentiates the usage of indentured servants and slaves, before and after Cromwell's conquest of Ireland. Because before Cromwell, indentured servants were treated fairly and they came with their own free will.

In addition, the term indentured servants is used for categorical purposes by politicians and researchers. Colloquially, the term servant is not commonly used. All decendants of redlegs in Barbados describe their ancestors as being 'brought as slaves'. Father Labat, a French priest who visited Barbados in the early 18th century, noted Irish indentured servants were commonly referred as 'white slaves'.[85]

Were the Irish black?

Irish people always had an ambiguous status wherever they went within the British Empire – politically, socially and legally. As the colonised population, they were considered inferior. According to the psychiatrist Denis Jackson, it was the British who viewed the Irish as black, 'not in the sense of physical pigmentation, but in the original pejorative sense of the Anglo-Saxon word for being dull and lacking in intelligence'. The Irish were often called 'white proto-slaves' or 'black men in white skins' to highlight the status of Irish indentured servants because they were classified more or less in the same way as slaves. Lerone Bennett Jr, American historian, the author of *the Shaping of Black America* wrote on the Irish indentured servants: 'They came, these Christian demi-slaves, the same way most blacks came, crammed shoulder to shoulder, toe to toe, the living and the dead side by side, in the unventilated holds of crowded ships. In this respect, as in others, there were striking similarities between the white servant trade and the black slave trade'.

In a letter to Roman Catholics addressing the wretched state of his 'countrymen', Anglo-Irish philosopher Bishop George Berkeley in 1735 wrote: 'The negroes in our plantations have a saying – If negro was not negro, Irishman would be negro'. When England tried to transport Irish indentured servants to Barbados, the local council quickly snapped: 'We desire no Irish rebels may be sent to us; for we want not laborers of that color to work for us'.[86] Irish people were often described as 'a profligate race,' 'white slaves,' and 'turbulent and dangerous' by the British.

In Ireland, the term 'Black Irish' has been used for many centuries as a description of people who had darker complexions with black eyes and black hair, like early settlers from Spain who were also called black Irish and the Vikings who were described as dark strangers. But when it is used outside of Ireland, it has different connotations. Generally, in Montserrat and Jamaica, the term 'Black Irish' developed on its own as it was used to describe an ethnicity whose lives were quite intertwined in many ways for centuries.

In popular culture, there is no shortage of such description. For instance, one of the most famous quotes is that of Irish writer Roddy Doyle, who famously placed a relationship between the Irish and Africans (African-Americans) and the hierarchy within Ireland that has always been existed, in his 1987 novel *The Commitments*:

> – The Irish are the niggers of Europe, lads. They nearly gasped: it was so true.
> – An' Dubliners are the niggers of Ireland. The culchies have fuckin' everythin'. An' the northside Dubliners are the

niggers o' Dublin.
– Say it loud, I'm black an' I'm proud.

Punishments

Servants and slaves worked together and lived side by side and both were often punished for a 'laugh'. Enslaved people often received horrific punishments unimaginable such as burning alive, gibbeting, decapitation and castration, while indentured servants were typically whipped but did not receive such extreme penalties for committing petty crimes. If servants left the plantation without permission from their master, more time was added to their term of indenture as a punishment, while African slaves were beaten. If slaves assaulted their master, they were whipped or killed, while servants were never killed for the same offence. As an ultimate punishment, indentured servants were normally kicked out of the island they were living on, transported to other Caribbean islands, such as Jamaica, or banished.

Servants were treated worse

According to various witness accounts, during the early plantation period, some servants, essentially Cromwell's victims, were apparently treated worse than slaves. Ligon observed that some masters made Irish servants work harder than African slaves as they only worked for a short period of time. In the 1650s, Irish indentured servants were prodded with sticks if they were too slow to work and often beaten with a cane around the head till the blood started flowing. If they complained about something, they were beaten and if they resisted, their time got doubled. Joseph Williams questioned in his book *Whence the Black Irish of Jamaica*: 'Such was the fate of the Irish victims of Cromwellian brutality, whether we wish to call them slaves or designate them by the more euphemistic name of bond-servants'.

Slavery-like conditions

The Irish servants were still under the same laws that governed European servants. However, that didn't mean Irish servants suffered less. The word slave is also used as a verb to describe horrific working and living conditions. In this sense, the term is applicable to many Irish indentured servants as the majority of them literally lived like a slave and died early. Father Antoine Biet, a French priest who visited Barbados in 1654 witnessed that some of the families, particularly so-called prisoners of war, convicts or general political prisoners, were forcefully split up on arrival and sold to different planters as a punishment. The servants and slaves lived and worked alongside each other in similar dreadful conditions. Food and clothing were always scarce but they ate slightly different food, wore different clothes and had different sleeping arrangements. Because of such atrocious treatment and poor living conditions, it was not uncommon for them to die before their indentures were expired, or even before their indentures were started, on the ship or on arrival after enduring the long inhumane journey. On top of this, Irish people were more vulnerable in the tropics than African people as they were not used to the hot climate and not immune to tropical-diseases. Because many Irish servants died early, planters eventually concluded that they were not fit to work in sugar plantations long term. They were not a suitable investment.

Holding arms

Planters in Barbados were distrustful about Irish servants holding arms, although almost 2,000 Irishmen were in the army of Barbados in 1667. Only in cases of emergency, enslaved Africans joined in the militia but they were never allowed to use firearms. According to the 1661 slave code, overseers could search 'negro houses' and if they found clubs and wooden swords, they could confiscate and burn them.

Religious freedom

Although Catholicism was officially forbidden in the British West Indies, the servants already had their own religion and a choice to choose their own faith, while slaves had no right to have a religion in the first place. According to Richard Ligon, the planters didn't allow their slaves to be Christians because of the English laws. 'I promised to do my best endeavour; and when I came home, spoke to the master of the plantation, and told him, that poor Sambo desired much to be a Christian. But his answer was, that the people of that island were governed by the lawes of England, and by those lawes, we could not make a Christian a slave. I told him, my request was far different from that, for I desired him to make a slave a Christian. His answer was, that it was true, there was a great difference in that: but being once a Christian, he could no more account him a slave, and so lose the hold they had of them as slaves, by making them Christians; and by that means should open such a gap, as all the planters in the island would curse him. So I was struck mute, and poor Sambo kept out of the Church; as ingenious, as honest, and as good a natur'd poor soul, as ever wore black, or eat green'.

Quakers were anti-slavery pioneers. The early Quakers in the British West Indies contained a handful of people from Ireland who typically owned slaves as it was a common practice. However, they quickly became staunch abolitionists. They made various attempts to give religious instructions to their slaves or to purchase slaves to make them free but the English promptly imposed various laws against Quakers. Just like Catholics, they were marginalised people within the British West Indies. The majority of Quakers eventually had to leave the Caribbean islands in the end.

Irish planters' maltreatment

Irish people's involvement with slavery was quite widespread although it may not be well-documented. Many planters and overseers were Irish themselves and some of them treated all workers atrociously. According to Father Biet who witnessed: 'One day I went to visit my Irishman. He had in irons one of these poor Negroes who had stolen a pig. Every day, his hands in irons, the overseer had him whipped by the other Negroes until he was all covered with blood. The overseer, after having had him treated thus for seven or eight days, cut off one of his ears, had it roasted, and forced him to eat it'. In order to discipline the slaves in 1693, Montserrat enacted 'An Act to restrain the Insolence of Slaves and for preventing them from committing any Outrages, as also the better ordering such Slaves'.[87] Any slave who stole anything worth 12 pence or more was to be put to death, when it was less, his or her ears were to be cut off and a severe whipping administered; anyone who found a negro more than forty feet off the footpath had the right to shoot and kill; in 1693, a black man Peter Boone who was convicted of the theft of nine pigs were cut into pieces and displayed on the public paths; a black slave who had almost beaten his overseer to death was suspended in chains and was to be given no food or water until he died. According to Akenson, the Irish who were 'overwhelmingly Catholics, rich, middling, and just above white-trash-poor bought into this system and all did so'.[88] In Montserrat, they were more apt to own slaves than were the British.

Irish people, both wealthy and former servants, were involved with the lucrative African slave trade. Generally, the Irish were active slavers who were keen to make substantial profits working independently or for the Royal African Company (RAC). One of the most famous Irish Catholic slavers was William Ronan, an officer of the RAC who actually worked in Ghana from 1687 to 1697, as well as some high profile slave merchants based in Nantes, France such as the Walshes, the Riordans and the Roches, and many others were based in Bristol and Liverpool. They justified themselves by saying that Africans who were shipped as slaves were prisoners of war so they would have been killed if they had not been shipped as slaves, amongst other reasons.

In any case, Donald Akenson, the author of *If the Irish Ran the World: Montserrat, 1630-1730* wrote that the Irish were avid slavers. 'At all levels of society the Irish were more apt to hold slaves than were the British, and yes, that the Irish were, on average, bigger slaveholders than were the British, but that at the very top – the very largest plantations where the Irish were overrepresented – this social structure ensued because a bunch of apostate Irish had become Protestant (and, therefore, somehow become tinctured with vice)'.[89] To sum up, Irish people were legally not slaves even though some were treated like slaves. They were given all sorts of monikers and considered as non-white until they were on the side of the British and part of England/Britain.

What was the role of Ireland in the British West Indies?

Ireland played a significant role within the British West Indies in expanding and establishing the British Empire. The most visible function was that it provided human capital – labour force, colonial administrators, lawmakers, planters, soldiers, merchants, artisans, sailors, privateers, priests, amongst other professions. People who directly benefited from the servant and slave trade were ship owners, merchants, agents, plantation owners, provision-related business owners, banks and finance houses that lent money to finance voyages. Ordinary people in Ireland also depended on the trade since more provision- and trade-related jobs were created locally such as packaging, distilling and milling. They were the most valuable Empire builders as they contributed to various industries back home in Ireland and England. Their economic activities made Britain extremely wealthy and also the Atlantic trade had an overwhelming impact on the economy, politics and society of Ireland and Irish people directly and indirectly.

Labour force

One of the main functions of Ireland was to offer a labour force. Ireland exported tens of thousands of indentured servants. They were the greatest asset and the backbone of the British colonies as they were part of developing plantations and infrastructure. The settlers and sojourners from Ireland had various social backgrounds and held different positions who were ubiquitous in every social stratification from planning to execution.

Soldiers

From its inception, Irish soldiers had been serving in the British army in all corners of the globe. Soldiers were highly mobile populations. Not just geographically but it was not uncommon for them to change sides or switch allegiance. Quite often, former soldiers ended up in the Caribbean independently to work or were forcefully transported from Ireland or elsewhere as indentured servants.

Irish soldiers in the Caribbean often fought in mainland America and other regions for or against Britain, or both. Some Caribbean islands changed hands several times, while other islands were divided into two parts by different European colonisers. As soldiers of foreign armies or privateers, the Irish were often against the English and eagerly helped French and Spanish colonisers to let them take over. Although Irish soldiers were scattered across the world and played a decisive role in helping to expand the British Empire (and American Empire), at the same time they had an equally crucial part in hindering their imperial dreams. The root cause of the military diaspora stemmed from British rule and colonisation in Ireland so there were obviously consequences on Britain. In some cases, the money the Irish made in the Caribbean was used as funds for the next rebellion against England back home or elsewhere.

Provision trade

Ireland largely provided various trading activities for the British West Indies and mainland American colonies. Under trade regulations constructed in London, Ireland was the chief supplier of provisions particularly heavily salted meat packed tightly in firkins and barrels to endure the tropics. The Irish provisions for the victualing of ships and the export of goods to British and non-British colonies increased along with the growing slave trade.

By the mid-17th century, Ireland had been steadily exporting a large quantity of salted beef, pork, butter, herrings, pickled tongues, bread, cheese, candles and low-priced linen clothes particularly for the labouring population in the British West Indies. Ships were filled with sugar and other colonial items and Irish Americans in the North American mainland colonies exchanged sugar and other colonial products, most of which was carried to London and the English outports first.

Irish agriculture and its provision-related industries benefited more directly from demand in the British West Indies than their counterparts in England. Irish merchants were highly visible in London and the English outports who managed to re-export sugar to Ireland. Trade with the British West Indies was considered as intercolonial commerce which means all trading activities were meant to profit England, the mother country. Ireland's position was more like a partner rather than subordination as evidence shows that Ireland economically grew significantly between 1660 and 1783, although the wealth was not shared exactly equally with the whole population of Ireland. After 1730, Ireland experienced a relatively peaceful and prosperous period, gradually increasing its population which reached 3.25 million in 1740.

The Atlantic trade opened up whole new prospects for local people. Thanks to the robust provision industries, growth and development were clearly visible in Irish ports, port cities and towns. Even agriculture performed better than other European countries during this period. Dublin and Cork were also transformed because of the trade with raw materials such as muscovado sugar, a wet brown sugar. The cane needed to be crushed and the juice boiled on the plantations. Then, it needed further refining in Europe before consuming. During the height of the trade, two thirds of sugar in Ireland was refined in Dublin. Almost all of the colonial items such as sugar, lumber, wheat and iron needed to be imported directly or indirectly into Ireland and those were prepared as products for final markets. The money and savings from Ireland regularly flew into the colonies via the Irish American trade. Because of these lucrative trade activities, some people took advantage and emigrated to the Middle Colonies, four of the 13 colonies in mainland America, and subsequently helped develop the whole region. Irish people were extremely well-connected and working ubiquitously for trading houses and commerce-related industries in London, various cities of the British Isles, mainland America and the Caribbean.

In exchange for exporting linen and provision food items, Irish merchants imported flaxseed, wood, wheat and flour from mainland America, and rum, sugar, tobacco and other tropical items from the Caribbean. There were more than 180 vessels registered between 1735 and 1776, in addition to the 78-owned in partnership with firms in Ireland.

Slave merchants

Slave merchants often began their slave trade career as slave ship captains or crew in the first place. Irish ports were also benefitted from the slave trade, along with English ports of London, Bristol and Liverpool. Originally developed as a port for Ireland in the Middle Ages by and for Irish merchants, Liverpool is known as the Irish city. Liverpool had been a vibrant Irish port, long before it started dominating the British slave trade. Because of its proximity, many of them settled there but newcomers from Ireland had always been present in Liverpool. One of Liverpool's earliest slaving voyages was made by *The Blessing* which sailed for Africa in 1700. Its owners, Thomas Johnson and Richard Norris ordered the captain to collect provisions at Kinsale and then take 'the first fair wind for the Guinea coast'. Later in the 18th century, slave ships from Liverpool sailed round the north of Ireland in order to bypass French pirates.

On board, there were always captains and crew with Irish surnames. For example, John Teague made five voyages from 1724 to 1727 and their captains were called Barry and Roach, common Irish names. In the 1720s, master of Bristol slaves, William Barry organised nine voyages. Michael Callaghan made a total of six voyages. The numbers of slaves were 1,036 out of his four voyages. In a separate occasion, he transported 280 slaves as a merchant from Callaghan and Co. David Tuohy from Tralee became a merchant after being a captain. Amongst 49 slave ship captains from Bristol that made voyages from 1785 to 1794, 40 captains were local and six were from Ireland.[90] Although there is no breakdown of 'local', Irish people are often included in this obscure classification. Locals in Liverpool and Bristol typically contained Irish people. All captains and crew preferred to work as merchants because it was extremely dangerous to be on slave ships. The death rate on slave ships was intensely high, estimated to be more than a quarter who died during the voyage.[91]

Since medieval times, Irish people had been trading with France as they had been sailing to St Malo, trading hides, beef and butter in exchange for wine. With the arrival of James II's defeated army, the Irish mercantile community expanded in France. When the French slave trade was steadily expanding between 1715 and 1740, Irish people there took part in it and eventually settled in Nantes, Bordeaux and La Rochelle that were known as slave and sugar ports. Quite a few of them had a flair for the trade and made a fortune. Profits made in the slave trade were used to buy chateaux in France, to establish more sugar plantations and various businesses across the world. They all had their family members based in French colonies of the Caribbean and mainland America.

When the Royal African Company, or RAC, an official British slaving company, was established in 1672, only the people who worked for the company could trade with slaves. According to protocol, Ireland was banned from slaving for the most part of the 18th century and Irish ports were officially banned from direct voyages to Africa. When the RAC lost its monopoly at the end of the 17th century, individual merchants who were based in England were able to join the trade. The most important English ports for slavery as the direct instruments of the trade were London, Bristol and Liverpool. From the decline of the RAC until 1740, Bristol was Britain's principal slaving port, and then eventually Liverpool started dominating the trade. The Frekes, the Callaghans, the Teagues, the Coghlans and the Connors were notable slave merchants based in Bristol, while the Dorans, the Butlers, the Ryans, the McGauleys, and the Tuohys were prosperous merchant families in Liverpool.

In the British West Indies, there were less restrictions on Irish people. Irish slave merchants were ubiquitous such as the Skerrets, the Ryans and the Tuites who were vigorously trading slaves from British ships and re-exporting them, along with cargoes of provisions from Ireland. Some of them were not only trading slaves in the British West Indies but in other non-British territories as well.

Some Irish people didn't officially belong to the British enterprises or other European counterparts but made a living as independent slave merchants in Cape Verde, a major slave trade centre that is 350 miles off the coast of Senegal, West Africa which was used as a bustling slave trading port. As they were not bound by Portuguese regulations, they purchased slaves directly from local merchants. In the 1740s, there was a leading

Irishman called Conel who functioned as an agent for Portuguese and English slave traders in the Cape Verde islands. They were not working for the Portuguese only but also for Dutch ships and merchants purchasing slaves directly from local merchants in Africa.

An English politician William Gladstone justified the slave-related trade as being beneficial to Ireland: 'The unrestricted commerce of the world would give employment to Ireland; her population would then exchange idleness and rags for industry and comfort; her fine streams, now wasting their powers, would give motion to numerous manufactories; her grain and provisions, now compelled to seek a market in other countries, would then find ample demand amongst her own improved population'.

Because the profits from the slave trade were considerable, England made enough money to fund industrialisation. Due to the industrial revolution that started in 1760 in England, there were abundant employment opportunities for all people, including Irish people in Britain and Ireland. Through trade and colonisation, capitalism began in England in the early and mid-1600s. The transatlantic slave trade that created enough capital eventually led to the rise of capitalism.

Turning into English

The general Catholic population were staunch opponents of Britain. They fought for Catholic France and Spain or attacked British ships as independent pirates, and later many of them became a part of the anti-slavery movement. On the other hand, once leaving Ireland, it was not uncommon for Irish people to start behaving and acting like the English, or to become more English, just like Oliver Cromwell expected. Cromwell and English officials believed that by removing local people from Ireland, it would eventually result in producing a large number of Englishmen or/and Protestants. Cromwell wrote in 1655 that once in the West Indies, the Irish would turn into Englishmen. Historian Nini Rogers agrees that they integrated rather smoothly: 'This proved to be true of the most successful of the Creole generation. William Stapleton's family changed religion and flowered as Oxfordshire gentry. Also from Nevis, the Tipperary Tobins saw their grandson James set out on a triumphal recrossing of the Atlantic to found the Bristol sugar firm of Pinney and Tobin (1783-1806)...In eighteenth century Jamaica the appointment of Irishmen to the highest legal offices became something of a tradition. Archdeacons, Fearons and Bourkes took this route, surrendering their Catholicism and acquiring wealth in land and slaves, setting their progeny on a trajectory for Eaton, Oxford and Westminster and the social delights of England's West Country'.[92]

The linen trade had an enormous impact on Belfast and clearly divided the north and the south within the island of Ireland. The gap between the rich and the poor widened and economic growth delivered benefits mainly to those already well-off. William Gladstone, the British statesman wrote: 'In contemplating the state of Ireland, cannot fail to remark the immense superiority of the condition of the north as compared with the South. The employment afforded by the linen trade in the north is an obvious cause of this superiority, and points out to us a practical remedy for the distress of the other parts of that country'. Subsequently, it also divided their political culture into two factions. The North became more and more English. A substantial amount of money was made from the Atlantic trade but only certain people got richer and impoverished people remained where they were. Even though, the majority of Irish people abroad were rather mobile and adaptable and often moved up the social ladder.

Whitening agent

Spanish colonies often planned to make their slave colonies less

African, or in other words less black. Spain used Irish people as a whitening agent in Hispaniola, Cuba and Puerto Rico, amongst other Spanish territories. For example, it is recorded that Irish people were used as part of the plantocracy's whitening scheme in Cuba. In 1835, more than 300 Irish people arrived to work as railroad labourers in Havana and they were effectively used for the scheme.

Overall, the Irish played remarkably diverse roles in the Atlantic trade. But not without those who paid the ultimate price. According to a historian Edmund Morgan, American freedom was developed along with the institution of slavery. Although some are critical of his analysis as there are other complex factors, freedom of the Americas couldn't have evolved without the sufferings of enslaved populations. In this sense, the Irish were a fundamental part of this fabric in the context of the British West Indies. They were all-rounders and the most important asset of the British Empire. Even though the Caribbean didn't become the final destination for the majority of Irish people, their legacy still clearly lives on.

Did the Irish end slavery?

Irish people who were involved with the slave trade became the friends of kings and the wealthy. The transatlantic slave trade provided wealth, work and consumer goods.

It was simply too lucrative to stop it even though there were always a small minority of abolitionists who believed in the injustice of enslavement. There are many factors that contributed to the abolition of slavery in the Americas. Some of the major reasons against the slave trade were: it was simply too risky to keep slaves and to maintain economic stability as there were slave revolts on a regular basis; slave-based goods were not lucrative anymore as the industrial revolution in England began; anti-slavery societies and religious groups such as the British and Foreign Anti-Slavery Society put pressure on inhumane practices; the growth of free trade ideas; overproduction of sugar in British colonies made the sugar prices low; political changes in England; the slave abolition movement became very active in various countries which sped up the abolition of slavery worldwide.

Apprenticeship

The Slavery Abolition Act was passed in 1833 and it took effect in 1834. However, Britain did not free slaves immediately. Instead, they introduced a new system called 'apprenticeship'. The British authority rationalised that slaves were not used to being independent and needed to learn how to be free. The new system was applied to teach freedom followed by a 4 or up to 8-year so-called apprenticeship period. In fact, the term apprenticeship was just a different name of slavery.

For example, below are some legal cases on how apprentices were treated by white employers from various Journals of the Stipendiary Magistrates of December 1836 in Barbados.

G.R. Doyle (complainant) vs Eight males, fifteen females (defendant)

Complaint: Indolent performance of labor

Decision: To perform three days extra labor

Will. A. Moore (complainant) vs Nine predial apprentices, (five women and four men) (defendant)

Complaint: Idleness

Decision: the men to work one Saturday each, the women two.

R. W. Harding (complainant) vs Eighteen apprentices, four males and fourteen females (defendant)

Complaint: The Manager being sworn, convicts the prisoners by deposing that their general conduct is exceedingly idle and

that chiding them for their improper conduct avails nothing.
Decision: All to work three Saturdays.[93]

During this period, they continued to work a 45-hour week without pay in exchange for living expenses provided by the plantation owners. But some British West Indian colonies such as Antigua and Bermuda didn't adopt the apprenticeship system. Those islands instantly freed their slaves as planters knew that it was cheaper to pay a daily wage to freed waged labourers than to keep them as apprentices as they had to offer food and housing. The apprenticeship system finally ended in 1838 and approximately 750,000 slaves throughout the British West Indies became free. When slavery was finally abolished, the British government agreed to pay 20 million pounds in compensation to 3,000 slaveholders throughout the British West Indian colonies for the emancipation of their slaves.

Catholic emancipation

The movement for Catholic emancipation which involved removing and reducing many of the restrictions on Roman Catholics in Ireland and other British Isles, and African slave emancipation developed in parallel. The British authorities dealt with both issues throughout the early 1800s. The Irish Act of Union in 1800 abolished the Irish Parliament which existed since the 13th century and united the Kingdom of Great Britain and the Kingdom of Ireland to create the United Kingdom of Great Britain and Ireland. The passing of Catholic emancipation in 1829 paved the way for the emancipation of the slaves. The complete emancipation of slaves, after the apprenticeship system finished, finally took effect in 1838.

Abolitionist movement

Before the slave trade was abolished throughout the British Empire, various campaigns to abolish slavery were launched.

Abolition meant that the actual buying and selling of slaves was made illegal. Once a respectable institution, why did slavery become unacceptable? Many pro-slavery people justified it as totally acceptable. Some of the reasons were: it was completely natural that some people were slaves as part of God's plan; it was written to obey their masters in the Bible; without slavery, it would threaten the structure of society; slavery was a useful form of punishment; living in slavery was better than poverty; they deserved to be enslaved because they were inferior beings; slavery had been around for centuries throughout most of human history; it was found in every civilization and had been practiced by different cultures and religions, amongst other reasons.

Because Britain did not want to give up the system, various attempts were made to justify slavery, especially from an economic point of view. For instance, in his correspondence, John Gladstone, a Scottish politician and slave merchant wrote to James Cropper, an English abolitionist: 'The cotton trade not only giving full employment to the population of the districts in England but since the removal of some absurd regulations in the last session of parliament, we have seen with delight some branches of this trade extending to Ireland and presenting the best means of improving and raising her depressed population'.

In fact, the majority of people were pro-slavery at the beginning of the abolitionist movement because they just took it for granted as the accepted social system. It was extremely hard and even dangerous to go against the stream as countless people were making a living or had a vested interest in the trade directly and indirectly. So who were actually against slavery? Because people in Ireland had been mistreated by England and the country had been ruled by England for such a long time, did they naturally know what it meant to be oppressed and did they have a sense of justice? Did the Irish actually influence the abolition of slave trade?

Abolitionists

At the beginning of the 5th century, Patricius, later becoming Saint Patrick, was kidnapped at 16 by raiders in Wales and sold as a slave in pagan Ireland. Patrick, coming from the Romano-British slave-owning clans, eventually became a bishop in Ireland and converted the local population. After the Romano-British warlord Coroticus kidnapped and killed many of Patrick's Christian converts, he wrote a letter to Coroticus and the British Christians to condemn him for enslaving Irish people and selling them to non-Christians, and calling on him to return the captives. This is one of the oldest existing anti-slavery documents.

During the 18th century, it was not uncommon for there to be anti-slavery activists in Ireland. Some symbolic historical figures who played a major part in the anti-slavery movement included Daniel O'Connell, Richard Robert Madden, Richard Allen, the second Marquis of Sligo and a group of middle-class women, most notably Mary Ann McCracken and Maria Edgeworth.

A distinguishable advocate and one of the most notable Irish nationalist leaders in Irish history is Daniel O'Connell (1775-1847). Born near Cahirciveen, County Kerry, he is affectionately called the Liberator and the Emancipator, and mostly known for his achievement of Catholic emancipation. A lawyer by training, he was profoundly concerned about human rights issues in Ireland. In order to petition for Catholic emancipation, he formed a nationwide series of mass meetings against the law. In 1823, he established the Catholic Association and shortly many professionals, lawyers, Irish priests and educated Catholic laymen joined the cause and became members. Once Catholic emancipation was achieved in 1829, he immediately started focusing on campaigning for a repeal of the Act of Union that was created in 1800 between Great Britain and Ireland. While he was campaigning, he got into trouble with authorities and got arrested. In prison, he wrote a letter dedicated to Irish Americans to take leadership of the anti-slavery cause in America.

The Liberator of Irish Catholics was also influential in the anti-slavery movement. His efforts were recognised in Britain, the Caribbean and mainland America. According to O'Connell, Irish MPs had played a major role in the parliamentary decisions to end slavery. O'Connell often mentioned that Ireland's anti-slavery traditions dated back to the time of St. Patrick who fought for human rights. At the Clare election in 1828, he asked the audience whether Irish Catholics were like 'negroes to be lashed by their drivers to the slave market and sold to the highest bidder'. He reiterated that Irish people were lovers of liberty and always felt a special affinity with oppressed peoples. O'Connell made a compelling statement in 1832: 'I am for speedy, immediate abolition. I care not what caste, creed, or colour, slavery may assume. I am for its total, its instant abolition. Whether it be personal or political, mental or corporal, intellectual or spiritual, I am for its immediate abolition. I enter into no compromise with slavery; I am for justice in the name of humanity and according to this law of the living God'. What he reiterated again and again was 'We did not want blood-stained money'. He also noted the Irish people were 'crawling slaves' and strongly condemned cruel Irish people for supporting the slavery cause in the West Indies and the North American mainland. In 1823, he joined the British and Foreign Anti-slavery Society. William Wilberforce, an English politician who became the voice of the abolition movement in Parliament, was one of the founding members. O'Connell visited Westminster as a staunch supporter of the abolition of slavery.

O'Connell was hugely inspired by the English Quaker abolitionist James Cropper when he came to Ireland in 1824. Cropper outlined a scheme in order to free the slaves in the Caribbean first, and then the North American mainland, and improve conditions in Ireland. His scheme was supported by O'Connell's Catholic Association. From that moment, O'Connell started focusing on the similarities between the conditions of the

Irish and African slaves. In 1830, O'Connell formed the Repeal Association, a political movement to campaign for a repeal of the Acts of Union of 1800 between Great Britain and Ireland. The Repeal movement was an attempt to liberate the oppressed Irish as well as to abolish slavery abroad.

During his journey of anti-slavery movements, Frederick Douglass (1818-1895) was a huge influence on him. Douglass is one of the most inspirational figures in the cause and the most significant African American leader of the 19th century. He lived 20 years as a slave and nearly nine years as a runaway slave. After publishing his own book *Narrative of the Life of Frederick Douglass, An American Slave,* he sailed to England and then visited Dublin. Because a Quaker abolitionist agreed to publish an Irish edition of his book, he planned to visit Ireland for a few days but ended up staying there for four months. Apparently, Ireland was an eye opener for Douglass. When he came to Ireland in 1845, just a few months before the Great Famine began, he truly felt a freeman for the first time. Why? Because Douglass instantly felt empathy towards local people upon setting foot in Ireland. As a long-term colony, Catholic people in Ireland had been oppressed just like black people had been oppressed in America. The abolitionist Douglass was genuinely shocked and distressed to see poverty in Ireland and destitute local people. Douglass also agreed to speak at a Repeal meeting in Conciliation Hall in Dublin. O'Connell introduced Douglass as 'the black O'Connell of the US'. Just like O'Connell, he was a great public speaker. He brought some instruments of torture and confinement used daily in the US such as shackles and irons to show the audience. Slavery was finally abolished in the US in 1865.

In his book, Douglass described his encounter with Irishmen when he was a slave in America. And the meetings left him with an unforgettable lasting impression. He wrote: 'I went one day down on the wharf of Mr. Waters; and seeing two Irishmen unloading a scow of stone, I went, unasked, and helped them.

When we had finished, one of them came to me and asked me if I were a slave. I told him I was. He asked, 'Are ye a slave for life?' I told him that I was. The good Irishman seemed to be deeply affected by the statement. He said to the other that it was a pity so fine a little fellow as myself should be a slave for life, He said it was a shame to hold me. They both advised me to run away to the north; that I should find friends there, and that I should be free. I pretended not to understand them; for I feared they might be treacherous. White men have been known to encourage slaves to escape, and then, to get the reward, catch them and return them to their masters. I was afraid that these seemingly good men might use me so; but I nevertheless remembered their advice, and from that time I resolved to run away'.

Another Irish man to dedicate his life to the anti-slavery cause was Richard Robert Madden, also known as R.R. Madden, (1798-1886) from Dublin. He was an historian of the United Irishmen and Catholic. A physician by training, he worked as a surgeon in London before but gave up his profession for the cause and went to the Caribbean. Because the Slavery Emancipation Act was passed in 1833, he decided to get involved with the great work of humanity. He came to Jamaica in November 1833 as he secured an appointment as special magistrate. Lord Mulgrave, Sligo's liberal predecessor as governor posted him to Kingston.

In order to make sure of compliance with the 1833 Emancipation Act, special magistrates were sent to the British West Indies. On behalf of the British government, Madden tried to impose anti-slavery rules in Jamaica. He wrote that when he arrived in Jamaica, he faced 'intense hostility from planters' harbinger which was considered an appropriate introduction for persons holding the appointments'.

Upon returning to London, he published *A Twelvemonth Residence in the Island of Jamaica* in 1835 which became a milestone in the anti-slavery movement. He wrote that the apprenticeship system, or also called indentured apprenticeship, was slavery in another form which prompted the government to form a select committee that included Daniel O'Connell 'to inquire into the working of the apprenticeship system in the colonies'. He also wrote that the system was a failure which offered 'no security for the rights of the negro, no improvement in his intellectual condition'. Madden's observation contributed significantly to the early abolition of the apprenticeship system in 1838. He subsequently went to Cuba to find out more about the Amistad affairs and Gambia to conduct more investigation. He pointed out that as long as slavery exists, it was impossible to fully utilise the vast resources of Jamaica.

An Irish university political economy professor in Dublin and Galway, John Elliott Cairnes (1823-1875) also published a pioneering book in 1862 *The Slave Power: Its Character, Career and Probable Designs: Being an Attempt to Explain the Real Issues Involved in the American Contest*. In his book, he criticised slavery as an ineffective labour system. He lectured on the causes of slavery and the origins of the Civil War in America. A Catholic Dowell O'Reilly from County Louth was a prominent politician, and a staunch advocate of Catholic Emancipation in Ireland, and the Attorney general and Magistrate in Jamaica. During the time of the apprenticeship system, he was called a 'fearless advocacy of the negroes'. American anti-slavery campaigners who were travelling through Jamaica in 1837 described him as 'one of the ablest men in the island'. Madden was hugely influenced by him as he served under him. Madden described him as a fearless advocate of the negroes' rights.

Educated at Eton and Cambridge, the Anglo-Irish first Marquess of Sligo, John Denis Browne (1756-1809) was a supporter of Catholic emancipation. As his grandfather married Elizabeth Kelly, daughter of Denis Kelly, a former chief justice of Jamaica, he inherited his Jamaican estates through family connections. In honour of Lord Sligo, a free settlement Sligoville was established in the north of Spanish Town in 1835. After the

Slavery Abolition Act of 1833, Jamaica immediately introduced the apprenticeship system. For example, domestic and non-praedial workers needed to serve for four years and field workers for six years without receiving salary. He was sympathetic to slaves during the period of apprenticeship.

James Kelly was one of the Ulster Presbyterian agents who handled linen and Irish provisions in the ports. After spending 17 years in Jamaica working as a bookkeeper and tradesman, Kelly published a book called *Voyage to Jamaica and Seventeen Years' Residence in That Island* in 1838 and wrote his first-hand accounts about the atrocious conditions of the slaves: 'In the month of March, 1814, having consulted neither friends nor friendly advisers, but my wayward disposition, I paid twenty guineas for a passage in the ship Hugh Crawford – took my portmanteaux on board in Belfast Lough, and a week after, was at anchor in the Cove of Cork, in the midst of upwards of one hundred sail of merchantmen, assembled to join convoy, it being war-time'. From Britain, it took six weeks to get to Barbados, where all ships stopped before leaving for Jamaica which took a further week. He wrote when he saw black people for the first time: 'In Bridgetown, the capital, I was disgusted with the appearance of the white Creoles I saw. The contrast between our rosy cheeked selves and them produced an extempore feeling of exultation. I was, however, pleased, when again on board, to see dozens of canoes come alongside with fruits, &c. I was struck with the shining faces of the Negroes – faces like polished ebony, and teeth, from the contrast with their black skins, so pearly white. I was astonished to learn that they were the slaves of the same haggard-looking Creoles I had been so shocked with. There is a lesson in this, I thought, and I resolved that I would be no slave-owner'. He witnessed injustice and felt deeply shocked and disgusted. 'With respect to the present state of the Negroes, I can say nothing of my own knowledge but from numerous authenticated accounts, I am persuaded that they are still enduring oppression more grievous to be borne than I ever witnessed in the time of slavery. It is true, they now see a definite period, in the place of illimitable bondage. Many bereavements and additional modes of coercing labour, with punishments of new introduction, are exhibited in these accounts, as the tread-mill, &c'.

Similarly, Benjamin McMahon also lived in Jamaica for 18 years and published a book called *Jamaica Plantership: Eighteen Years Employed in the Planting Line in that Island* in 1839. He initially left Ireland in 1818 as a soldier for the Colombian Army to liberate local people from Spain. All soldiers in the Irish Legion supporting Bolivar's campaign suffered atrocious hardships in Venezuela under their commander, notorious Wexford man John Devereux. As a result, the majority of soldiers deserted and moved to nearby Jamaica. McMahon and his comrades were 'so dissatisfied with our treatment by the commanders, that many of us threw up our engagements, and became scattered about. I, together with about 200 others, determined to go to the West Indies; and we sailed for Jamaica in the beginning of June 1820'. Typical Irish soldiers all found slavery unacceptable. In his book, he summed up what he thought: 'First, as a friend of civil and religious liberty, I abhor slavery in my very soul: knowing, as I do, that no man has a just right to deprive his fellow-man of his property, of his limbs, or of his life except for some crime against society. Secondly, I regard slavery in all its forms, and under all the modifications it has assumed, as calculated to deprive its victims of those habits and energies, which are necessary to effective and beneficial labour. Thirdly, I am anxious to expose the treachery, the torture, and the tyranny, practised by the overseers and attorneys of Jamaica, towards the slaves, and even in many instances towards the bookkeepers, by such a succinct detail of facts as my experience and observations for the last eighteen years may enable me to supply'. In Marguerita, an island of Venezuela, he first confronted the brutal facts. 'My ignorance of the nature of slavery in those days, left me entirely at a loss to know how all the black inhabitants could have received such horrible wounds; and the truth never struck me till after I had been a little time in Jamaica. The people about forty years old were grey-headed, emaciated, worn-down and often deformed, occasioned by the barbarous cruelty of the inhuman Spaniards, calling themselves Christians…The book-keeper told me I was a fool to notice the overseer's actions – if he were to kill, burn, and destroy the people, I should say nothing about it; and if the overseer had the slightest idea of my observations, he would instantly discharge me, and leave me unable to get another berth'. Although a large majority of Irish people felt disgusted at the horrendous treatments of slaves as they were flogged severely just for a laugh, they went with the stream. He witnessed that slaves were flogged without mercy and 'Several of the slaves had iron bands about their necks, and were chained together in pairs with long chains, and were made to work in this way from morning till night'. Apparently, those who were against slavery faced a similar ethical dilemma. 'Whenever I have met with a tyrant, whether he were friend or foe, I have always felt as though the great black devil had crossed my path, and that I was bound as the friend of liberty and humanity notwithstanding the guise he wore, to exhibit his cloven hoof, and to hold up his delinquencies to public execration'. In the end, McMahon decided to leave Jamaica, as he intended 'to do justice to every class of society there, connected with slavery; so far as truth would bear me out'. He was well aware that it was extremely risky to write a book exposing true events as many names were scattered throughout the book. Kelly and McMahon were obviously horrified with plantation life where slaves were treated inhumanely and decided to be catalysts by telling what they saw and experienced. Irish people like them who finally left the Caribbean typically didn't return to Ireland but London.

Religious and other organisations

Quakers and Protestants were the principal movers behind the Irish anti-slavery movement. Anti-slavery meetings were often held in churches and religious halls. There were no Catholic groups that got involved with the anti-slavery movement. While Protestant dissenters preferred gradual abolition with a laid back approach, the Quakers, or the Religious Society of Friends, were the first white people to openly criticise slavery and called for its immediate termination. That's why they were considered as dangerous fanatics.

They were known for their humanitarian approach through charity and peace building work and their entrepreneurship, as they set up various businesses, such as milling, textiles, shipping, imports, exports, food and tobacco production, brewing, iron production and railways industries throughout Ireland. At the beginning, like everybody else, Quakers embraced slavery as the existing social system. However, things changed when the founder George Fox actually travelled to the Caribbean in 1671, spoke against slaves' poor treatment in Barbados and declared: 'To be sober and to fear God...their masters and overseers will love them and deal kindly and gently with them'.

Quakers in the Caribbean tried to spread their religious message to their slaves but soon legislation was adopted to limit their activities. In Barbados, for example, there was a law forbidding them to take their slaves to Quaker meetings in 1676 but they ignored the warning which resulted in another stricter law being passed in 1678. In Nevis, slaves were placed in irons for attending their meetings. It was commonly considered that enlightening slaves was extremely dangerous. Active Quakers and missionaries were eventually removed and shipped elsewhere. During a Quaker meeting held in London in 1761, it was decided that all slave owners and slave traders be expelled from the Society. In May 1787, the Committee for the Abolition of the Slave Trade was founded in London. Nine of its 12 founding members were Quakers who functioned as a central organisation to coordinate with local activists. Particularly, Quakers in mainland America were actively involved with anti-slavery movements. In 1791, they started a campaign to boycott products made and produced by slave labourers. In 1836, Joseph Sturge, a Quaker from England came to Jamaica to thoroughly investigate the situation of former slaves there. After he wrote an extremely critical report, he launched the British and Foreign Anti-Slavery Society in 1839. Between 1820 and the 1860s, the Underground Railroad (Quakers were extensively involved with the series of routes and safe houses by which slaves were helped to escape) was extended to the Caribbean. Sturge also spent ample time in Montserrat where he purchased the Elberton Sugar Estate to grow limes and to prove that free labour functioned better.

During the height of the anti-slavery movement, numerous non-religious organisations and groups existed. There were anti-slavery societies in Belfast, Dublin, Waterford, Cork, Youghal and Limerick. By 1824, the foundation of the Dublin Association for Endeavoring to Promote the Mitigation and Gradual Abolition of Slavery in the British Colonies existed. Just like in Britain, nonconformist Protestants led the group and meetings were often held in Protestant halls and chapels. The Dublin Anti-Slavery Society was founded in 1827 which had close ties with the Anti-Slavery Society based in London. The Dublin-based Hibernian Negro's Friend Society (HNFS) was founded in 1829 by Charles Orpen, a Protestant physician from Cork. And later, it was re-structured and organised as the Hibernian Anti-Slavery Society (HASS) in 1837. The three men travelled to London to press parliament for the abolition of apprenticeship with 75,000 Irish female signatures. The society called for the immediate ending of slavery.

In those days, women in Ireland were excluded from parliamentary politics and quite a few middle-class women formed ladies' groups and keenly participated in the movement.

For example, the Hibernian Ladies Negro's Friend Society was founded in 1833. The Dublin Ladies' Anti-slavery Society began in 1837. There were various activities in cooperation with England-based organisations such as the Birmingham Ladies Anti-slavery Society that brought similar activities to Dublin and Tralee. Women were involved with all aspects of campaigning from raising funds to organising local committees. They were generally very good at calling attention to the situation by being creative and inspirational. Maria Edgeworth wrote a story *The Grateful Negro*, while the Quaker Mary Birkett penned her *Poem on the African Slave Trade*. Mary Ann McCracken from Belfast was a supporter of the anti-slavery movement from its early days when the United Irishmen called for a boycott of sugar products from the West Indies. She was a founder member of the Women's Anti-Slavery Society in Belfast. She used to correspond with R.R. Madden and once wrote: 'I am both ashamed and sorry to think that Belfast has so far degenerated in regard to the Anti-Slavery cause'.

The lover of the oppressed?

It was the Quakers who actively started the anti-slavery movement in Ireland. The movement had spread and become common throughout the island of Ireland by the late 18th century. When William Wilberforce, the MP for Hull started campaigning to abolish the slave trade, Quakers in Dublin tried to organise meetings and to vote to support his cause. But they were not able to find enough sympathisers to participate in it because almost all Irish companies were directly and indirectly involved with the slave economy. In a desperate attempt, they asked the public to stop buying sugar so that it would free the slaves. A leading United Irishman, Thomas Russell was librarian of the Belfast Library and Society for Promoting Knowledge (the Linen Hall Library) from 1794 to 1796. He wrote a letter to the people of Ireland on the present situation of the country which mentioned the abolition of slavery. James McDonnell, a pioneer physician from Belfast also called for the abolition of slavery and for Catholic emancipation. Within Ireland, Belfast residents had the strongest voice for slavery. For example, when Waddell Cunningham from Belfast, the founding president of the Belfast Chamber of Commerce, had a plantation in Dominica and he named it Belfast. He tried to set up a slave company in Belfast, but failed as he met strong opposition.

While local sentiment in Ireland strongly supported Catholic emancipation and the call for the abolition of slavery, those Irish people who were part of the economic activity namely merchants, slave owners, affluent planters and officers openly supported it. People earned a living and some became extremely well-off and powerful on the proceeds of slavery as commercial and industrial advances in Ireland were linked to the slave and provision economies in the Caribbean.

Indeed, Daniel O'Connell helped Catholics to win the right to become members of parliament and then played a significant part in the English parliament. But in fact, the majority of Irish MPs actually voted against the early abolition of apprenticeship, according to the *British Emancipator* published in 1838. Seeing the picture as a whole, the Irish were not the main catalysts who ended slavery. In those days, the large majority of the population in Ireland were still struggling to make ends meet. Although a broad range of abolitionist groups were operating all across Ireland, their activities were confined to the middle class and didn't go beyond the community level.

Epilogue

Looking up to the seemingly endless range of the blue mountains of Jamaica, the first thing that came to my mind was: I would definitely have gone up there if I were enslaved. I may have been living vicariously through all the people who were featured in this book as I immersed myself in the subject for a while. But no mountains have ever given me a sense of freedom and reassurance before.

The geographical contrasts between Jamaica and Barbados are striking. Barbados initially developed in a distinctive way because of its unique location. This island was the first port of call of all ships in the Caribbean after crossing the Atlantic. Because Barbados is relatively flat and small, it was not ideal for someone who wanted to run away and/or hide after plotting revolts although it didn't stop them from conspiring and escaping. Instead, the most rebellious troublemakers were deported to various islands, particularly Jamaica, the westernmost British island, as a punishment. The distance between the two islands is about 2,000 km (1,230 miles), so it took a few days by boat from Barbados to Jamaica in those days. Upon arriving, many – both servants and slaves – plotted revolts and fled into the mountains. In terms of numbers, there were more former slaves up on the mountains who eventually formed their own settlements but quite a few runaway Irish were living amongst them. In many ways, Irish servants and African slaves played corresponding parts within the British system.

Stuart Laycock, the author of *All the Countries We've Ever Invaded: And the Few We Never Got Round To* wrote that the British have invaded almost 90 per cent of the countries around the globe at various times. With or without purpose, the Irish always travelled with the British. As I witnessed more and more about their fragmented legacy in the Americas, I was constantly reminded how the large majority of people left Ireland full of anger, bitterness and in despair and also how they influenced and shaped politics in the British colonies. There is no doubt that Britain could have quickly secured more Caribbean territories if it was not for a countless number of Irish fighters (and informers) who were on the French and Spanish sides. What would have happened if Britain hadn't obtained an overwhelming number of Irish soldiers when they invaded Jamaica? Britain could have won the American Revolutionary War if it had more supporters on its side. If it was not for Ulster Presbyterians from Ireland, American independence probably could have not been achieved. If a highly skilled Irish soldier in the British Army Edward Despard and his revolutionary force which comprised of Irish soldiers, sailors and labourers had been a little bit more successful, he could have seized the Tower, the Bank of England and ultimately power in London. And the list is endless. Considering a score of highly successful Irish generals and officers at large existed throughout European Armed Forces along with accomplished merchants with lucrative contacts, when looking at the much larger context of European imperialism, the Irish were pretty much part of it too.

More than three centuries have passed since the first Irish indentured servants were a prominent feature in the Caribbean, its current residents are predominantly black people. But you can still clearly see, hear and feel some Irishness in Montserrat and some parts of Jamaica (Although it could be depending on the people you meet in certain localities, I didn't particularly feel it in Barbados, Antigua and St Kitts). Not only visible street signs, surnames, Irish towns and place names can be seen throughout the Caribbean to varying degrees but shows from within, for example, in the way they carry themselves. Many researchers have identified an Irish brogue and words in the local colloquial language as well as some other cultural features.

In researching this book, I've visited various places throughout the Caribbean and I spent more time in the Caribbean's Irish island, Montserrat. Although the volcano eruption in 1995 changed the demographic and psychological landscape forever, what I find incredibly fascinating is the way they banter and gossip which made me feel like I was at times in Cork or Kerry. Within a few minutes of a conversation in a shop, on the bus, or at the bus stop, the people I met (mostly older generations) all said something to remember, added something funny or wise to finish the conversation. For instance, what random strangers said to me during a brief conversation is (I quickly jotted down each time): Keep your head up; the next minute, you are gone; Live in the present; always look out; it is not the end of the world, it is not the judgment day today, relax, I promise you tomorrow will be just fine; life is full of difficulties that will only make you strong, and so on. At first, local people are not overly friendly and open, but rather, they will initially give you a sceptical look if you keep talking to them. But you will soon realise once they open up, they can be very chatty. They are not direct and they tend not to give you straightforward answers. They have the gift of storytelling. Another thing I noticed was the community spirit. Because it is a close-knit society, Montserrat is a very safe place. Because everybody knows everybody, when someone is struggling or needing help, local people are always willing to help. There is definitely a community need to help each other. Local funerals last a long time, up to a few hours. Lots of people turn up. Until recently, a viewing was common, so I have been told. After the service, they eat goat water (a stew that has originated in Ireland). I came with an open mind but I find Jamaican Patois intriguing. I don't think the Irish are 100% responsible for their current accent because so many other factors are intertwined, not to mention Jamaica is also being globalised. But the Irish influence on their language is unmistakable. I even imagined they could be on the same wavelength with the Irish. British comedian Lenny Henry who has Jamaican parents once described Ireland as 'Jamaica in the cold'.

Because Ireland has been always a diverse society, its people have never been homogenous. So at the various archives, it is always interesting to see how Irish people are buried or missing in the name of categorisation. (Not to mention, changing status, positions, names, allegiance, religions along the way adding more confusion.) Because British West Indian islands are Anglican, it is not always straightforward to find information on Catholic people and the people with other denominations as they were somewhat marginalised. According to the Anglican records, non-Anglican people are often grouped as 'Catholic', 'Jewish', 'others', or not registered at all. At the archives, the files that cannot be categorised are often written or put under the 'others' category. The Irish, especially the indentured servants or/and Catholic people's information is often put in this category or doesn't even exist. (Consequently, their wills and inventory at death are easier to find. This explains that they had become more British by the time they died) Sometimes the Irish have a special classification for themselves depending on different time periods and islands/regions. The Irish in England and in the British system continuously had this unclassifiable position and status. It is very hard to pinpoint them because their information is often missing or badly categorised.

So could this be the reason why Irish people in the Caribbean are forgotten and ignored? Regarding the Irish who had been living in Barbados for centuries, Dr. Tadhg Ó hAnnracháin, Head of the School of History and Archives, University College Dublin, was quoted in the TG4's documentary *The Redlegs: Ireland's Sugar Slaves of Barbados* on the reason why the topic is not widely known: 'I suppose there isn't a lot of information on that subject. Irish historians don't talk about it very often. It isn't taught in schools or universities'. But could it also be the shame factor in that Ireland were involved in the servant and slave trade? It is said that history is written by the winners.

Are there no winners in this Irish story during this particular period of time, perhaps? Is that because the majority of them were working behind the scenes and successful Irish people had eventually become British? In 2018, the first ever famine film *Black 47* was released. The film director Lance Daly said in an interview with the *Irish Times* the reason why it had taken 170 years to tell the story in a big screen: 'It's hard to find a story you can tell that the audience can bear sitting through. When you do attempt it you realise why. It's impossible to portray the suffering'. Indeed, a people's history is more complicated to write than political or military history. The majority of them may be lost in the annals of history as the passive participants of the Empire builders but in fact they were fundamental in every aspect of Britain's imperial past.

The Irish Diaspora is extraordinary unique. It was not a one-time event in history. This relatively tiny island continuously exported an astonishing number of people throughout the centuries. After all, the Caribbean was the first region in the world where forced displacement of the Irish on a massive scale took place. The last large-sized migration that is still fresh in our memory happened during the 1980s when 206,000 people (mostly highly educated) left Ireland. Spanning different time scales and involving diverse individuals, the Irish Diaspora is like a massive database. That's why it can be used as a screening device to interpret a wide range of subjects, race, ethnicity, class, gender and social inequality. Certainly, there are similarities with the Green and Black Atlantic, albeit to varying degrees. The Irish slave myth is an indispensable tool to counterbalance, explain or even justify inequality. Samuel Clemens, or more widely known as Mark Twain, once wrote: 'History doesn't repeat itself, but it often rhymes'. A huge interest in the topic in the recent years probably means that history may be rhyming.

Acknowledgements

I am grateful to all those people from all walks of life who have helped me over the years as I have been researching the Irish Diaspora in the Caribbean on and off for more than two decades. I've visited and conducted research in the UK, USA, Ireland, the Netherlands, Barbados, Jamaica, Antigua, St Kitts and Nevis, Montserrat, Cuba, Puerto Rico, Suriname and Cape Verde. I owe much to the staff of various libraries and archive collections. The archival staff and librarians at the following institutions provided invaluable assistance: The National Archives at Kew, London; The British Library, London; The Library of the Society of Friends, London; The Postal Museum, London; The National Army Museum's Templer Study Centre and Archive, London: The Friends Historical Library, Dublin; the Church of Ireland RCB Library (Robert Gallagher); the Irish Capuchin Provincial Archives (Brian Kirby); the National Maritime Museum of Ireland (Richard McCormick); The National Archives, the Hague, Netherlands; The National Maritime Museum Library, Amsterdam; The Leiden University Library; the National Archives of St Kitts and Nevis; The National Library, St Kitts and Nevis; The Montserrat Public Library; The National Archives, Antigua; the National Archives, Jamaica (Kimberly Blackwin); the National Library of Jamaica; Shilstone Memorial Library, Barbados Museum & Historical Society, Barbados (Dario Forte and Harriet Pierce); the Barbados National Archives. I ran into Woodwill Marshall and Matthew Reilly at the archives in Barbados and I am grateful for their advice and suggestions.

Endnotes

1. Carlyle, *Oliver Cromwell's Letters and Speeches with Elucidations,* p169
2. Godkin, *The Land War in Ireland 1870,* p225
2. O'Callahan, *To Hell or Barbados,* p55
3. Linebaugh, *The Many-Headed Hydra,* p120
4. O'Callaghan, *To Hell or Barbados,* p14
5. Morgan, *Slavery and the British Empire,* p14
6. Linebaugh, *The Many-Headed Hydra,* p121
7. Rogers, *Ireland, Slavery and Anti-Slavery,* p27
8. Smith, *Colonists in Bondage,* p167
9. O'Callaghan, *To Hell or Barbados,* p80
10. Gribben, *Puritans and Catholics in the Trans-Atlantic World 1600-1800,* p39
11. O'Callaghan, *To Hell or Barbados,* p79
12. Williams, *Whence the Black Irish of Jamaica,* p4
13. Linebaugh, *The Many Headed Hydra,* p123
14. Sheppard, *The Redlegs of Barbados,* p20
15. Smith, *Colonists in Bondage,* p215
16. Beckles, *White Servitude and Black Slavery in Barbados 1627-1715,* p68
17. Smith, *Colonists in Bondage,* p238
18. O'Callaghan, *To Hell or Barbados,* p125
19. Smith, *Colonists in Bondage,* p293
20. Graag, *Englishmen Transplanted,* p127
21. Graag, *Englishmen Transplanted,* p127
22. Sheppards, *The Redlegs of Barbados,* p76
23. McCartney, *The World of Daniel O'Connell,* p176
24. Beckles, *White Servitude and Black Slavery in Barbados 1627-1715,* p122
25. Miller, *Emigrants and Exiles,* p144
26. Miller, *Emigrants and Exiles,* pp144-145

27. Sheppard, *The Redlegs of Barbados,* p19
28. Beckles, *White Servitude and Black Slavery in Barbados 1627-1715,* p84
29. Amussen, *Caribbean Exchanges,* p69-70
30. Smith, *Colonists in Bondage,* p290
31. Morgan, *Banishment in the Early Atlantic World,* p63
32. Beckles, *White Servitude and Black Slavery in Barbados 1627-1715,* p102
33. Shepperd, *The Redlegs of Barbados,* p23
34. Chinea, *Irish Indentured Servants, Papists and Colonists in Spanish Colonial Puerto Rico,* p171
35. Coke, *A journal of the Rev. Dr. Coke's Fourth Tour,* p182
36. Watson, *The Civilised Island, Barbados,* p104
37. Reilly, *At the Margin of the plantation: Alternative Modernities and an Archeology of the 'Poor Whites' of Barbados,* p97
38. Donnell, *Caribbean Irish Connections,* p55
39. Watson, *The Civilised Island, Barbados,* p110
40. Sheppard, *The Redlegs of Barbados,* p82
41. O'Callaghan, *To Hell or Barbados,* p102
42. Beckles, *White Servitude and Black Slavery in Barbados 1627-1715,* p118
43. Beckles, *White Servitude and Black Slavery in Barbados 1627-1715,* p120
44. A Collection of the State Papers of John Thurloe, p508
45. Miller, *Emigrants and Exiles,* p141
46. Edmundson, *A Journal of the Life, Travels, Sufferings and Labour of Love in the Work of the Ministry,* p297
47. Durham, *Caribbean Quakers,* p13
48. Rogers, *Ireland, Slavery and Anti-Slavery,* p3
49. Truxes, *Irish-American Trade,* p44
50. Truxes, *Irish-American Trade,* p45
51. Madden, *Twelvemonth's Residence in the West Indies,* p303
52. Beckles, *White Servitude and Black Slavery in Barbados 1627-1715,* p161

53. Akenson, *If the Irish Ran the World,* p119
54. Shaw, *Everyday Life in the Early English Caribbean,* p116
55. Shaw, *Everyday Life in the Early English Caribbean,* p107
56. O'Callaghan, *To Hell or Barbados,* p109
57. O'Callaghan, *To Hell or Barbados,* p115
58. O'Callaghan, *To Hell or Barbados,* p115-6
59. https://www.globalresearch.ca/the-irish-slave-trade-the-forg otten-white-slaves/31076
60. Linebaugh, *The Many-Headed Hydra,* p123
61. Watson, *The Civilised Island, Barbados, A Social History 1750-1816,* p106
62. Williams, *Whence the Black Irish of Jamaica,* p53
63. Linebaugh, *The Many-Headed Hydra,* p273
64. Linebaugh, *The Many-Headed Hydra,* p254
65. Linebaugh, *The Many-Headed Hydra,* p248
66. Akenson, *If the Irish Ran the World,* p121
67. Dyde, *A History of Antigua,* p53
68. Dyde, *A History of Antigua,* p53
69. Rogers, *Ireland, Slavery and Anti-Slavery,* p62
70. Gragg, Larry, *Englishmen Transplanted,* p188
71. Williams, *Whence the Black Irish of Jamaica,* p44
72. Linebaugh, *The Many-Headed Hydra,* p126
73. Rogers, *Ireland, Slavery and Anti-Slavery,* p42
74. Akenson, *If the Irish Ran the World,* p31
75. Akenson, *If the Irish Ran the World,* p45
76. Akenson, *If the Irish Ran the World,* p95
77. Akenson, *If the Irish Ran the World,* p185
78. Robertson, *Gone is the Ancient Glory: Spanish Town, Jamaica 1534-2000,* p39
79. Curtis, *Nothing but the Same Old Story: The Roots of Anti-Irish Racism,* p29
80. Stewart, *Memoir and Correspondence of Viscount Castlereagh, second Marquess of Londonderry* p417
81. Rogers, *Ireland, Slavery and Anti-Slavery,* p45

82. Williams, *Whence the Black Irish of Jamaica,* p74
83. Chenoweth, *Simplicity, Equality and Slavery: an Archaeology of Quakerism in the British Virgin Islands,* p36
84. Rogers, *Ireland, Slavery and Anti-Slavery,* p54
85. Beckles, *White Servitude and Black Slavery in Barbados,* p230
86. Beckles, *White Servitude and Black Slavery in Barbados,* p236
87. Akenson, *If the Irish Ran the World,* p142
88. Akenson, *If the Irish Ran the World,* p149
89. Akenson, *If the Irish Ran the World,* p145
90. Rogers, *Ireland, Slavery and Anti-Slavery,* p96
91. Rogers, *Ireland, Slavery and Anti-Slavery,* p96
92. Rogers, *Ireland, Slavery and Anti-Slavery,* p65
93. Sturge, *The West Indies in 1837,* xxvii

References

Unpublished theses

Brehony, Margaret, 'Irish Migration to Cuba, 1835-1845: Empire, Ethnicity, Slavery and 'Free' Labour' (unpublished PhD thesis, The National University of Ireland, Galway, 2012)

Daniels, Jason, 'Atlantic Contingency: Jonathan Dickinson and the Anglo-Atlantic World, 1655-1725' (unpublished PhD thesis, The University of Warwick, London, 2013)

Kennedy, Maria, 'The Religious Society of Friends (Quakers) in Ireland: Sectarianism and Identity' (unpublished PhD thesis, The University of Birmingham, 2016)

Kopytoff, Barbara, 'The Maroons of Jamaica: An Ethnohistorical Study of Incomplete Polities, 1655-1905' (unpublished PhD thesis, the University of Pennsylvania, 1973)

Reilly, Matthew, 'At the Margin of the plantation: Alternative Modernities and an Archeology of the 'Poor Whites' of Barbados' (unpublished PhD dissertation, Syracuse University, 2014)

Riach, Douglas, 'Ireland and the Campaign against American Slavery 1830-1860' (unpublished PhD thesis, University of Edinburgh 1975)

Watson, Karl, 'The Civilised Island, Barbados, A Social History 1750-1816' (unpublished PhD thesis, The University of Florida, 1975)

Wayne, Tomich, 'Prelude to Emancipation: Sugar and Slavery in Martinique 1830-1848' (unpublished PhD thesis, The University of Wisconsin-Madison, 1978)

Books and Articles

Akenson, Donald, *If the Irish Ran the World: Montserrat, 1630-1730* (Kingston, 1997)

Amussen, Susan, *Caribbean Exchanges: Slavery and the Transformation of English Society, 1640-1700* (Chapel Hill, 2007)

Anderson, Eileen, 'An Alternative View to the Propaganda: The Irish-American Press and the Spanish-American War', *Irish Migration Studies in Latin America* (November 2007), pp 163-170

Bartlett, Thomas and Jeffery, Keith., (eds.), *A Military History of Ireland* (Cambridge, 1996)

Beckles, Hilary, *A History of Barbados from Amerindian Settlement to Nation-State* (Cambridge, 1990) Beckles, Hilary, 'A riotous and unruly lot: Irish Indentured Servants and Freemen in the English West Indies, 1644-1713', *The William and Mary Quarterly*, vol. 47, no.4 1990, pp. 503-522

Beckles, Hilary, *White Servitude and Black Slavery in Barbados 1627-1715* (Knoxville, 1989)

Besson, Jean, *Martha Brae's Two Histories: European Expansion and Caribbean Culture-Building in Jamaica* (London, 2002)

Bielenberg, Andy, *The Irish Diaspora* (London, 2000)

Binasco, Matteo, 'The Activity of Irish Priests in the West Indies: 1638-1669, Irish Migration Studies in Latin America', *Society for Irish Latin American Studies*, vol 7 no 4. November 2011.

Bishop, Matthew, *The Political Economy of Caribbean Development* (Basingstoke, 2013)

Black, Clinton, *History of Jamaica* (London, 1965)

Black, Jeremy, *The Atlantic Slave Trade in World History* (New York, 2015)

Blight, David, (ed), *Narrative of the Life of Frederick Douglass, an American Slave, Written by Himself with Related Documents* (Boston, 2003)

Block, Kristen, *Ordinary Lives in the Early Caribbean: Religion, Colonial Competition, and the Politics of Profit* (Athens, 2012)

Block, Kristen, et al, 'Subjects Without an Empire: The Irish in the Early Modern Caribbean', *Past & Present*, February 2011, vol 210 Issue 1, p33

Brumwell, Stephen, *Redcoats: The British Soldier and War in the*

Americas, 1755-1763 (Cambridge, 2002)

Buckley, Roger, *Slaves in Red Coats: The British West India Regiments, 1795-1815* (London, 1779)

Burn, W. L., *The British West Indies* (London, 1951)

Burton, Gera, Liberty's Call: Richard Robert Madden's Voice in the Anti-Slavery Movement, *Irish Migration Studies in Latin America,* (November 2007), pp 199-206

Byrne, Thomas, 'Banished by Cromwell? John Hooke and the Caribbean', *Irish Migration Studies in Latin America,* (November 2007), pp 215-219

Canny, Nicholas, *Kingdom and Colony: Ireland in the Atlantic World 1560-1800* (Baltimore, 1988)

Canny, Nicholas, *Making Ireland British 1580-1650* (Oxford, 2001)

Capp, Bernard, *Cromwell's Navy: The Fleet and the English Revolution 1648-1660* (Oxford, 1989)

Carlyle, Thomas, *Oliver Cromwell's Letters and Speeches with Elucidations* (London, 1846)

Caron, Aimery, et al, 'Jean-Baptiste DuTertre on the French in St. Croix and the Virgin Island: A translation with Introduction and Notes', Bureau of Libraries, Museums & Archaeological Services, Department of Conservation & Cultural Affairs, occasional paper no. 4, 1978

Chenoweth, John, *Simplicity, Equality and Slavery: An Archaeology of Quakerism in the British Virgin Islands, 1740-1780* (Gainesville, 2017)

Chinea, Jorge, 'Irish Indentured Servants, Papists and Colonists in Spanish Colonial Puerto Rico, ca. 1650-1800', Irish Migration Studies in Latin America, (November 2007), pp 171-182

Coke, Thomas, *A journal of the Rev. Dr. Coke's fourth tour on the continent of America* (London, 1792)

Coupeau, Steeve, *The History of Haiti* (Westport, 2008)

Currie, Stephen, *Slavery* (San Diego, 1999)

Curry, Christopher, *Freedom and Resistance: A Social History of Black Loyalists in the Bahamas* (Gainesville, 2017)

Curtin, Philip, *The Atlantic Slave Trade: A Census* (Madison, 1969)
Curtis, Liz, *Nothing but the Same Old Story: The Roots of Anti-Irish Racism* (Nottingham, 1984)
Daly, Vere, *The Making of Guyana* (London, 1974) Delany, Francis, *A History of the Catholic Church in Jamaica B.W.I 1494 to 1929* (New York, 1930)
Dickson, David, *Old World Colony: Cork and South Munster 1630-1830* (Madison, 2005)
Doan, James, 'The Irish in the Caribbean' (1995) ABEI Journal, The Brazilian Journal of Irish Studies, no. 8 (June 2006)
Donnell, Alison, *Caribbean Irish Connections: Interdisciplinary Perspectives* (Kingston, 2015)
Duffy, Michael, *Soldiers, Sugar and Seapower: The British Expeditions to the West Indies and the War against Revolutionary France* (Oxford, 1987)
Dunn, Richard, *Sugar and Slaves: The Rise of the Planter Class in the English West Indies, 1624-1713* (Chapel Hill, 1972)
Durham, Harriet, *Caribbean Quakers* (Hollywood, 1972)
Dyde, Brian, *A History of Antigua: The Unsuspected Isle* (Oxford, 2000)
Dyde, Brian, *Out of the Crowded Bagueness: A History of the islands of St Kitts, Nevis & Anguilla* (Oxford, 2005)
Edmundson, William, *A Journal of the Life, Travels, Sufferings and Labour of Love in the Work of the Ministry, of that Worthy Elder and Faithful Servant of Jesus Christ, William Edmundson* (London, 1829)
Edwards, Dudley, *Daniel O'Connell and His World* (London, 1975)
Emmet, Thomas, *Ireland Under English Rule: A Plea for the Plaintiff* (London, 2009)
Fanning, Charles, *New Perspectives on the Irish Diaspora* (Carbondale, 2000)
Fitzgerald, Patrick, et al, *Migration in Irish History, 1607-2007* (Basingstoke, 2008)
Fergus, Howard, *Montserrat: History of A Caribbean Colony*

(Oxford, 2004)

Gal, Allon, (eds), 'The Call of the Homeland',IJS Studies in Judaica, Brill (March 2010)

Galenson, David, 'The Rise and Fall of Indentured Servitude in the Americas: An Economic Analysis', The Journal of Economic History, Vol. 44, No. 1 (Mar., 1984), pp. 1-26

Gladstone, John, et al, *Correspondence on the Present State of Slavery in the British West Indies and in the United States of America* (Shannon, 1972)

Godkin, James, *The Land War in Ireland 1870: A History For the Times* (London, 2010)

Gragg, Larry, *Englishmen Transplanted: The English Colonization of Barbados 1627-1660* (Oxford, 2003)

Gragg, Larry, *The Quaker Community on Barbados: Challenging the Culture of the Planter Class* (Columbia, 2009)

Gribben, C., et al (ed), *Puritans and Catholics in the Trans-Atlantic World 1600-1800* (Basingstoke, 2016)

Handler, Jerome, 'Escaping Slavery in a Caribbean Plantation Society: Marronage in Barbados, 1650s-1830s', KITLV Journals, New West Indian Guide/ Nieuwe West-Indische Gids 71 (1997), no: 3/4, Leiden, pp 183-225

Handler, Jerome, et al., *Contesting White Slavery in the Caribbean: Enslaved Africans and European Indentured Servants in 17th-century Barbados* (New West Indian Guide, 2016)

Handler, Jerome, et al., 'Father Antoine Biet's Account Revisited Irish Catholics in Mid-Seventeenth-Century Barbados', in A. Donnell (eds), Caribbean Irish Connections (University of the West Indies Press, Mona, Jamaica), pp. 33-46.

Haring, C. H., *The Buccaneers in the West Indies in the XVII century* (Hamden, 1966)

Hay, Douglas, (ed), *Masters, Servants and Magistrates in Britain an the Empire 1562-1955* (Chapel Hill, 2004)

Heartfield, James, *The British and Foreign Anti-Slavery Society, 1838-1956 A History* (Oxford, 2016)

Hinds, Hilary, *George Fox and Early Quaker Culture* (Manchester, 2013)

Hoffman, Michael, *They Were White and They Were Slaves: The Untold History of the Enslavement of Whites in Early America, Independent History* (Coeur D'Arlene, 1993)

Hourigan, Niamh, *Rule-Breakers: Why Being There Trumps Being Fair in Ireland* (Dublin, 2015)

Hurley, Michel (ed), *Irish Anglicanism 1869-1969* (Dublin, 1970)

Ignatiev, Noel, *How the Irish Became White* (London, 2008)

Inniss, Probyn, *Whither Bound St. Kitts - Nevis* (Basseterre, 1983)

Jeffery, Keith (ed), *An Irish Empire? Aspects of Ireland and the British Empire* (Manchester, 1996)

Jordan, Don, et al, *White Cargo: The Forgotten History of Britain's White Slaves in America* (Edinburgh, 2008)

Kenny, Kevin, (ed), *Ireland and the British Empire* (Oxford, 2006)

Kenyon, John (ed), *The Civil Wars: A military History of England, Scotland, and Ireland 1638-1660* (Oxford, 1988)

Kinealy, Christine, *Daniel O'Connell and the Anti-Slavery Movement: The Saddest People The Sun Sees* (London, 2011)

Lane, Kris, *Blood & Silver: A History of Piracy in the Caribbean and Central America* (Oxford, 1999)

Lane, Kris, *Pillaging the Empire: Piracy in the Americas* (London, 1998)

Lewisohn, Florence, *St. Croix under Seven Flags* (Hollywood, 1970)

Ligon, Richard, *A True and Exact History of the Island of Barbados* (London, 1970)

Linebaugh, Peter, et al., *The Many-Headed Hydra: Sailors, Slaves, Commoners, and the Hidden History of the Revolutionary Atlantic* (Boston, 2000)

McCartney, Donal, (ed), *The World of Daniel O'Connell* (Dublin, 1980)

McGarrity, Maria, *Washed by the Gulf Stream: the Historic and Geographic Relation of Irish and Caribbean Literature* (Newark,

2008)

McNicholas, Anthony, *Politics, Religion and the Press: Irish Journalism in Mid-Victorian England* (Bern, 2007)

MacRaild, Donald, *The Irish Diaspora in Britain, 1750-1939* (Hampshire, 1999)

MacRaild, Donald, (ed) *The Great Famine and Beyond, Irish Migrants in Britain in the Nineteenth and Twentieth Centuries* (Dublin, 2000)

Madden, R., *Twelvemonth's Residence in the West Indies during the Transition From Slavery to Apprenticeship* (Westport, 1835)

Maxwell-Stewart, Hamish, 'Convict Labour Extraction and Transportation from Britain and Ireland, 1615-1870', Global Convict Labour, 2015, vol 19, pp 168-196

Miller, Kerby, *Emigrants and Exiles: Ireland and the Irish Exodus to North America* (Oxford, 1985)

Miller, Kerby, et al (ed) *Irish Immigrants in the Land of Canaan: Letters and Memoirs from Colonial and Revolutionary America, 1675-1815* (Oxford, 2003)

Minz, Sidney, *Sweetness and Power: The Place of Sugar in Modern History* (New York, 1985)

Monahan, Michael, *The Creolizing Subject: Race, Reason, and the Politics of Purity* (New York, 2011)

Morgan, Edmund, *American Slavery American Freedom: The Ordeal of Colonial Virginia* (New York, 1975)

Morgan, Gwend, et al, *Banishment in the Early Atlantic World: Convicts, Rebels and Slaves* (London, 2013)

Morgan, Kenneth, *Slavery and the British Empire* (Oxford, 2007)

Mulcahy, Matthew, *Hubs of Empire* (Baltimore, 2014)

O'Callaghan, Evelyn, (eds), *Caribbean Irish Connections: Interdisciplinary Perspectives* (Kingston, 2015)

O'Callaghan, Sean, *To Hell or Barbados: The ethnic cleansing of Ireland* (Dublin, 2001)

O'Connell, Maurice, (ed), *The Correspondence of Daniel O'Connell, vol I 1792-1814*, (Dublin, 1972)

O'Connell, Maurice, (ed), *The Correspondence of Daniel O'Connell, vol VIII 1846-1847* (Dublin, 1980)

Ohlmeyer, Jane, 'Seventeenth-century Ireland and the New British and Atlantic Histories', American Historical Review, April 1999, pp 446-462.

O'Neill, Peter, (ed), *The Black and Green Atlantic: Cross-Currents of the African and Irish Diasporas* (London, 2009)

Orderson, J. W., *Creoleana and the Fair Barabadian and Faithful Black* (Oxford, 2002)

O'Shea, J. Murder, *Mutiny & Mayhem* (Dublin, 2012)

O'Siochuru, Micheal, *God's Executioner: Oliver Cromwell and the Conquest of Ireland* (London, 2008)

O'Siochuru, Micheal, *God's Executioner: Oliver Cromwell,* RTE factual TV programme,

Painter, Nell, *The History of White People* (New York, 2010)

Parish, Peter, *Slavery: History and Historians,* (New York, 1989)

Pepys, Samuel, *The Diary of Samuel Pepys, I – X* (London, 1970)

Pons, Frank, *The Dominican Republic: A National History* (Princeton, 1998)

Power, Orla, 'Beyond Kinship: A Study of the Eighteenth-century Irish Community at Saint Croix, Danish West Indies, Irish Migration Studies in Latin America', (November 2007), pp 207-214

Price, Richard, *The Convict and the Colonel: A Story of Colonialism and Resistance in the Caribbean* (Durham, 2006)

Rego, Marcia, *The Dialogic Nation of Cape Verde: Slavery, Language, and Ideology* (Lanham, 2015)

Rifkin, Jeremy, *Beyond Beef: The Rise and Fall of the Cattle Culture* (New York, 1993)

Robertson, James, *Gone is the Ancient Glory: Spanish Town, Jamaica 1534-2000* (Kingston, 2005)

Rodgers, Nini, 'The Irish in the Caribbean 1641-1837, an overview', Irish migration studies in Latin America, (November 2007), pp 145-156

Rodgers, Nini, *Ireland, Slavery and Anti-Slavery: 1612-1865* (London, 2007)

Shaw, Jenny, *Everyday Life in the Early English Caribbean: Irish, Africans, and the Construction of Difference* (Chapel Hill, 2013)

Sheppard, Jill, *The Redlegs of Barbados: Their Origin and History* (New York, 1977)

Sheridan, Richard, *Sugar and Slavery: An Economic History of the British West Indies 1623-1775* (Kingston, 1974)

Sloane, Hans, *A Voyage to the islands Madera, Barbados, Nieves, S.Christophers and Jamaica* (London, 1707)

Smith, Abbot, *Colonists in Bondage: White Servitude and Convict Labor in America 1607-1776* (Chapel Hill, 1947)

Smith, Adam, *The Wealth of Nations* (New York, 1994)

Stack, Liam, 'Debunking a Myth: The Irish were not Slaves, too', New York Times, 17 March 2017: Print.

Stewart, Robert, *Memoir and Correspondence of Viscount Castlereagh, second Marquess of Londonderry* (London, 1848)

Sturge, Joseph, *et al*, *The West Indies in 1837* (New York, 2007)

Thurloe, John, *A Collection of the State Papers of John Thurloe September 1655 to May 1656* (London, 1742)

Trevor-Roper, Hugh, *The Crisis of the Seventeen Century* (Indianapolice, 1967)

Truxes, Thomas, *Irish-American Trade 1660-1783* (Cambridge, 1988)

Vaughan, W.E., (ed), 'A New History of Ireland, Volume VI: Ireland Under the Union, II: 1870-1921', (Oxford, 2010)

Walvin, James, *Black Ivory: A History of British Slavery* (London, 1992)

Williams, Joseph, *Whence the Black Irish of Jamaica* (New York, 1932)

Wheeler, James, *Cromwell in Ireland* (Dublin, 1999)

Zacek, Natalie, *Settler Society in the English Leeward Islands, 1670-1776* (Cambridge, 2010)

HISTORY

Chronos Books is an historical non-fiction imprint. Chronos publishes real history for real people; bringing to life people, places and events in an imaginative, easy-to-digest and accessible way - histories that pass on their stories to a generation of new readers.

If you have enjoyed this book, why not tell other readers by posting a review on your preferred book site.

Beaten But Not Defeated

Siegfried Moos - A German anti-Nazi who settled in Britain

Merilyn Moos

Siegi Moos, an anti-Nazi and active member of the German Communist Party, escaped Germany in 1933 and, exiled in Britain, sought another route to the transformation of capitalism.

Paperback: 978-1-78279-677-0 ebook: 978-1-78279-676-3

A Schoolboy's Wartime Letters

An evacuee's life in WWII — A Personal Memoir

Geoffrey Iley

A boy writes home during WWII, revealing his own fascinating story, full of zest for life, information and humour.

Paperback: 978-1-78279-504-9 ebook: 978-1-78279-503-2

The Life & Times of the Real Robyn Hoode

Mark Olly

A journey of discovery. The chronicles of the genuine historical character, Robyn Hoode, and how he became one of England's greatest legends.

Paperback: 978-1-78535-059-7 ebook: 978-1-78535-060-3

Readers of ebooks can buy or view any of these bestsellers by clicking on the live link in the title. Most titles are published in paperback and as an ebook. Paperbacks are available in traditional bookshops. Both print and ebook formats are available online.

Find more titles and sign up to our readers' newsletter at http://www.johnhuntpublishing.com/history-home

Follow us on Facebook at https://www.facebook.com/ChronosBooks

and Twitter at https://twitter.com/ChronosBooks